C.D.

F2.5.87

COUP D'ETAT
A Practical Manual

Gregor Ferguson

COUP D'ETAT

A Practical Manual

ARMS AND ARMOUR PRESS

First published in Great Britain
in 1987 by Arms and Armour Press Limited, Link House,
West Street, Poole, Dorset BH15 1LL.

Distributed in the USA by Sterling Publishing Co. Inc.,
2 Park Avenue, New York, NY 10016.

Distributed in Australia by
Capricorn Link (Australia) Pty. Ltd., P.O. Box 665,
Lane Cove, New South Wales 2066, Australia.

British Library Cataloguing in Publication Data:
Ferguson, Gregor
Coup d'etat: a practical manual.
1. Coups d'etat – History – 20th century I. Title
321.09 JC494

ISBN 0-85368-761-7

Maps and diagrams drawn by David Gibbons.

Designed by David Gibbons; edited by Michael Boxall;
typeset by Typesetters (Birmingham) Ltd.; printed and
bound in Great Britain.

CONTENTS

MAPS AND DIAGRAMS

PREFACE

The coup d'état is as much a fact of political life today as taxes, hypocrisy and personal greed. A huge amount has been written about coups d'état; why they happen, what happens as a result of them, who they happen to and when, but nobody has yet looked at the coup d'état from the point of view of the military officer who must carry it out.

Textbooks on the subject of civil–military relations abound, primers on political and economic theory are two a penny and there is a constantly growing bibliography covering the political history of just about every country in the world. Very few books pay more than cursory attention to the way a particular coup was carried out, however. In the course of my research for this book I came across a standard work on the subject of the Portuguese revolution of 1974/5; interested, I scanned it eagerly for information about the planning and execution of the coup d'état which placed Spinola in power. I found it eventually – three pages of it, in a book of some 270 pages! The same thing happened when I found what I thought would be a useful text on Thailand's succession of coups d'état. This time there was even less information available. I confronted the same problem wherever I turned.

Slowly the truth began to dawn on me; there is no standard text on the subject of the coup d'état as a military operation. To be sure, no coup d'état takes place in a vacuum – obviously the way in which it is planned and carried out is a function of the political process which lead to it in the first place – but there must, surely, be guide-lines? The nearest I came to these were two slim volumes written by distinguished academics and to which I refer later on. For the most part it was necessary to draw my own conclusions and write my own rules from the information available.

Here was my second problem; the information available is so scanty that it was impossible to be certain of its accuracy. In the end I decided to concentrate on a few well-documented coups or attempted coups and try to work out the reasons for their success or failure in the context in which they were set. Would it be possible to apply elsewhere the lessons learned from one particular coup? Yes, I think it would – bearing in mind, of course, that no two coups d'état are exactly alike because the political conditions which lead to an attempted coup change from country to country and from time-frame to time-frame.

Certain factors remain constant. Displacing a government and either proclaiming one's own rule or putting a nominee into power is an exercise in control: control of the country; control of its rulers; control of the armed forces and control of the population. Leaving aside factors peculiar to specific countries, which would naturally affect one's planning and execution, there are rules governing the coup; it *can* be examined in part as a mechanical process; it *can* be studied as a military operation much like a commando raid or an airborne assault.

With this in mind, then, I have tackled the subject from the point of view of the plotter, whether civilian or military, faced with the problem of 'taking out' his or her own government. I have drawn on a number of examples of coups d'état which have taken place throughout the world in comparatively recent times. That some of these coups were successful and some not, is unimportant; I have chosen them not just for the quality of their documentation but for the lessons they provide. The one fictitious example on which I draw has a basis of truth which may be evident to those who are familiar with the major European city in which it is set, but no insult is intended towards the citizens, garrison or elders of the conurbation concerned!

If the citizens of the city in question do read this book, I shall be very pleased, for it is aimed at a lay (in military terms) readership. The coup d'état, being confined largely to Third-World countries, has become something of a joke. One is inclined to be overly dismissive of a country in which a coup d'état has taken place; coups occur in banana republics whose population expects nothing from its politicians and even less from its armed forces. People fail to realize what a complex operation a coup d'état can be and thus fail to give some recently successful plotter the credit for having carried it through. I hope this book helps to change that attitude.

The real-life examples from which I draw my lessons are all more or less accurately documented; I have chosen half a dozen or so (some of them abject failures) because they illustrate in greater or lesser form some of the problems the plotter faces. Being concerned more with operational than political matters I have tended to skate over some of the very real problems to which these coups were a reaction or which resulted from the coups concerned. I make no apology for this – other writers have covered the ground far better and in greater detail than I could hope to do, so I recommend that the reader who wishes to know more about the political background to a coup, and the subsequent fall-out, consult other works.

In conclusion, for the benefit of those who may accuse me of striking somewhat too cavalier an attitude towards the sacred principles of democracy, I would ask the reader to bear in mind, as I did, the words of General Sir John Hackett, writing in his standard text *The Profession of Arms* (Sidgwick & Jackson, 1983): 'What a society gets in its armed services is exactly what it asks for, no more and no less. What it asks for tends to be a reflection of what it is. When a country looks at its fighting forces, it is looking in a mirror; the mirror is a true one and the face that it sees will be its own.' With that thought in mind, and the author's judgement of political rights and wrongs temporarily suspended, let us carry on.

Gregor Ferguson, Wimbledon, February 1987

INTRODUCTION

Since the end of the Second World War there have been 311 attempted coups d'état, in some 79 separate countries, 170 of which have been successful. The most benighted country in this respect has been the Republic of Argentina, which has suffered no less than thirteen coups or attempted coups, and in two particular years (1955 and 1971) suffered no less than three in twelve months.

To put these figures another way, half of the sovereign states represented at the United Nations have experienced an illegal or unconstitutional overthrow of their existing governments (democratically elected or not) at some point in their recent history. A few of the countries which figure in these statistics have only a recent history – they did not exist as sovereign states until the 1960s or 1970s and in most cases have suffered more coups d'état than constitutional elections.

This book is about the way in which coups d'état are planned, organized and executed, and what it takes to make them work. Some excellent books have been written about the coup in general, sometimes as part of a broader study of civil-military relations, and two of these I commend to the reader: *The Man on Horseback* by Professor S. E. Finer, and *Coup d'Etat – A Practical Manual* by Dr Edward Luttwak. The present book, while bringing them up to date in one or two minor areas, is intended to complement them as the only practical handbook on the subject, written from the points of view of the planner and the officer charged with carrying out the operation.

A comprehensive study of the coup d'état should encompass five separate areas:

- **Motivation**
- **Opportunity**
- **Means**
- **Execution**
- **Aftermath**

Between them, Professor Finer and Dr Luttwak have produced the standard works covering Motivation, Opportunity, Means and Aftermath, but nobody, to my knowledge, has studied in any real depth the most crucial area of all – Execution. So, while acknowledging my debt to these two gentlemen, I must explain the manner of arrangement that I have adopted for this book.

The first Chapter deals with Motivation. Coups d'état do not happen spontaneously so it is necessary to know something of the driving force behind men and women who are prepared to risk imprisonment and worse in pursuit of an untimely change in the government of the day.

The Chapter on Opportunity, deals with the necessary prevailing conditions without which a coup is unlikely to be successful, and how these conditions can be either created or, if they exist naturally, exploited. The penultimate chapters deal with Execution: the ways and means of securing the apparatus of power and achieving a stranglehold on the country before, as discussed in the final chapter – Aftermath – consolidating one's constitutional grip, imposing authority and taking up the reins of government. They follow chapters dealing with Means. What does it actually take to displace the rulers of a particular country? This section looks at both the amount of force required and the agencies that can supply it, as well as at the levers which must be seized in order first to paralyze and then control the machinery of government.

But first two definitions.

COUP D'ETAT

A coup d'état is not a revolution, nor is it a guerrilla campaign, nor yet a simple mutiny in the armed forces. A revolution implies a mass uprising against a particular ruling class; the introduction of a new order, a catastrophic event in the nation's history. While a coup d'état may herald the start of a revolution, there is nothing 'popular' about it. It is (or should be) a swift, precise operation aimed at displacing the current rulers and replacing them with oneself or one's own nominees. One reason why the coup d'état is popular is because it is so quick; a revolutionary war could take a long time and, unless foreign backing is forthcoming from the start, or a significant number of the army desert to join one's cause, bringing their weapons with them, there is no guarantee that the war will succeed against the armed might of the state. Besides, even a successful revolutionary war will inevitably alienate at least part of the population (thus making the job of the loyalist security forces that much easier) and may result in serious long-term damage to an economy upon which one may soon have to rely.

A coup d'état, then, is simply a means of seizing power quickly and effectively within an existing framework so that, once established, one can either operate within that framework or start slowly to alter it. As such, the coup d'état is favoured equally by the forces of both right and left.

Political analysts will point out that it is not always necessary to mount a coup d'état in order to change things within one's own country. Professor Finer, in particular, has described the mechanism by which a powerful clique within a country can exercise influence, directly or indirectly, upon a ruling government without either seeking, or being forced, to supplant it. The threat of violence (all right, let us call it institutionalized intimidation) can be remarkably effective, as can the threat of a complete withdrawal of support from a government. The coup d'état in the Philippines in 1986 was an example of the latter, where elements of the armed forces, seeing which way the wind was blowing after the rigged elections and

President Marcos's disputed victory, withdrew their support from the head of state and transferred it to Mrs Corazon Aquino.

The Machiavellian politics and labyrinthine negotiations necessary to make such a course of action effective are no part of this book. We are concerned here with the real thing – the displacement, lock, stock and barrel, of a ruling government and its replacement with something manifestly different in composition, complexion and, possibly, political allegiance. In fact, this book is concerned with the worst-case scenario: a coup d'état organized and carried out in the face of stiff opposition and under conditions of great secrecy. Not all coups are carried out in this way, but by examining the worst case at all times, we can come to appreciate some of the problems faced by plotters in the past, and learn something about the conditions within a country – political, social and military – which make a coup d'état possible and affect for better or worse its chances of success.

THE GOVERNMENT

The government is what the coup seeks to change. A coup offers much more certainty than a general election, especially in an unsophisticated country or one where election malpractice is widespread. But beware! Even some of the least sophisticated countries are composed of power blocs remote from the government but on whose goodwill the government's authority depends – trades unions, for example, or major industrial organizations, or the Press. When talking about overthrowing a government one is talking also about neutralizing the effective power of these blocs to frustrate one's ambitions, either at the time or later. Thus, when talking about the 'Government' in this book it will be obvious where I am referring to 'the Establishment' in a wider sense. Any government, except those few which wield absolute power backed up by a monopoly of force, relies very much on consensus for its moral authority. The more politically sophisticated the state, the more scope there is for a non-governmental power group to challenge that authority and mobilize opinion against it. They could do the same to you after your coup.

It is not enough, therefore, simply to storm the presidential palace, throw the President into gaol and then proclaim one's supremacy. For the purpose of the coup itself (and perhaps only for a short while) it will be necessary to neutralize any agency that is in a position to oppose one's move, either by incarcerating its leaders, immobilizing its equipment, or by subverting its key personnel and making them part of the plot. If you can't be beaten, you may find some surprising people becoming your allies.

1
MOTIVATION

It is stupid to say of some recently successful coup-plotter that, 'He simply wanted power.' Many people want power. This is a part of human nature, and to ascribe a plotter's motives to one of man's more dominant psychological characteristics is to say nothing at all. The really interesting question is, what was it that so sharpened So-and-So's desire for power that he overthrew the president/king/prime minister, and seized it for himself?

The answer is usually much more complicated than the one given in the first sentence. Revolution is one motive; he wanted to create a new order but either couldn't wait to do so in a constitutional manner, working within the establishment, or would never have stood a chance of being voted into a position of power where he could have initiated the revolution from within the presidential palace. Alternatively, the government was already a revolutionary one, but so firmly established that, despite near-universal unpopularity, it was impossible for the opposition to change things constitutionally. Perhaps the president had eliminated the political opposition, or else had so altered the constitution that even a unanimous political movement could not legally displace him.

The revolutionary/counter-revolutionary motive is common, and leads to the widespread misconception that a coup d'état is, *de facto*, a revolution. This is manifestly untrue.

Another common motive is the one advanced by the armed forces of certain countries (notably in Latin America): a mission to 'Reform', to save the country from itself or from the decadence and frivolity of the politicians who may be accused of weakening or dissipating the national spirit or turning the country into what the fighting men perceive to be a laughing-stock. Equally, they might argue that the government's ineptitude or corruption has bled the economy dry and turned the nation into a sick joke on the international scene, and use this reason to justify their intervention. Sadly, there is often a great deal of justification for taking this course of action, especially in parts of Africa, Asia and Latin America.

Simple self-interest is as often as not a motive for mounting a coup d'état, though not, for obvious reasons, acknowledged as such. An army, or the armed forces in general, if they are particularly inward-looking and divorced from the mainstream of public thought, may see a simple cut in the nation's defence budget – even in times of national hardship – as a threat to the last bastion of stability, strength, honour and national spirit within the national borders. Or some power bloc, seeing what it perceives as an imbalance of power to the detriment of its own interests (it could be an unpopular political party, a militant tribal bloc, or the business community), may initiate a coup d'état or sponsor one by the armed forces if it does not have the power to mount one itself. Any perceptive reader will realize that, in particular circumstances, the motive stated for mounting a coup is an honest and honourable one, the results being justified by an improvement in the condition of both State and population, if not immediately then in the long term. Place yourself in the position of a Nigerian businessman who awoke on New Year's Eve 1983 to find that the President, for whom he may have voted not six months before, had been deposed and that a Major-General in the Nigerian Army was in the process of creating a Supreme Military Council which would rule the country in place of the President's own cabinet. What would have been his reaction? Disgust at the military? 'Oh, no! Not again!', perhaps? Wrong. Like most Nigerians he probably welcomed the action of the armed forces and the anti-corruption campaign and War Against Indiscipline (WAI) which followed.

Idi Amin of Uganda offers an interesting example of the self-interest motive in mounting a coup d'état. It will be remembered that he seized power during President Milton Obote's absence from Uganda at the Commonwealth Heads of State Conference in Singapore in 1971. Amin had achieved a reputation even then as something of a monster and his ambition knew no bounds. He had been recruiting Anyanya tribesmen (his own people, in effect) into the Ugandan Army in order to create his own power base; he was corrupt; he was a danger to Obote's Government and the President knew this. He also had little evidence to support his suspicions. Obote tried to draw Amin's teeth by promoting him sideways, from Army Chief of Staff, with direct control over the troops, to Army Commander. Finally, just before he flew to Singapore, Obote demanded an accounting from Amin as to why £2,500,000 of army money had gone missing, and why more and more armed robbers captured recently were in possession of army weapons and ammunition. these, and other factors, precipitated the coup, and Obote found himself in Singapore without a country and, apparently, without friends.

Contrast the Nigerian experience with the prospects for an Argentine liberal enjoying the political sunshine of President Alfonsin's administration. If the military, angered by his cuts in defence spending, insulted by his campaign to bring the perpetrators of the so-called 'Dirty War' to justice, humiliated and vengeful (and thus hypersensitive to perceived slurs on their honour) after a resounding defeat during the 1982 Falklands conflict, were to strike and assume power once again, how much peace of mind could the liberal enjoy? Especially if he was vociferous in his condemnation of military rule and the praetorianism of the armed forces of Argentina. Not much, one suspects.

All this goes to show that there is no such thing as a 'good' or a 'bad' coup. There may be a final reckoning on Judgement Day, but until then the justification and consequences for good or evil of a coup d'état remain very much a matter of subjective opinion. The United Nations notwithstanding, there is still no universally accepted code of human and institutional conduct. How can there be when one country allows the advertising of alcoholic beverages on television, while another flogs any citizen who even looks at the stuff? If this seems to the reader to be an abdication of the author's powers of judgement, even of his humanitarian principles, it is not.

Having explored some of the motives for a coup d'état, one cannot leave the subject without considering the effect these have on its aims. The primary aim, naturally, is to be successful, to place oneself or one's nominee in power; what then? Economic reform? Constitutional reform? Intensification of the campaign against the insurgents who have been showing up the previous government's inability to take effective action? An accommodation with the insurgents? Improvement (or termination!) of relations with the former colonial power, or aggressive neighbour? Expulsion of the Gastarbeiter, the illegal immigrants whose black market or legitimate employability is damaging the economy or infuriating the locals? Creation of a university so that the country can start producing its own doctors and engineers? Creation of a national defence-manufacturing industry? Or simply an end to years of human rights violations? Or is this the golden opportunity for your tribe or class to get its own back after years of persecution and discrimination?

Whatever the aim (and it may be any or none of these) it is important to get the right people on your side from the very start – at the planning stage, if possible. If, for example, the aim is economic reform intended to improve exports and the balance of payments to the greater benefit of the country as a whole (and, obviously, the government and industry in particular), it would be wise to seek the backing of the industrialists, especially (in a small country) if some of the more important ones are local chiefs of a foreign multi-national corporation whose presence in-country is vital to the economy. Some really cynical manipulation on their part (a threat to pull out because the government is corrupt or its policies wrong, for example) might help create the conditions required for universal acceptance of your presence in the presidential palace. The company might even pay to raise a force of mercenaries who can take over the country without your having to involve the armed forces. On the other hand, it may all go wrong; if national feeling is strong among the population, if the government is quite popular and if there is the slightest undercurrent of resentment against the multi-national concerned (Union Carbide in India, for instance), the government could tell the corporation to get lost, and good riddance, and might become all the more popular for doing so, however detrimental the outcome of this move might be.

Similarly, a new regime, committed to restoring what it perceives to be national pride, or some arbitrary national identity, or simply creating a national condition with which it feels more comfortable (and this is often the real reason for many military-inspired coups d'état), might be better off going to the middle and upper-middle classes (very few countries today have a genuinely aristrocratic tradition among their armed forces) and enlisting the support of leading elements such as the local business community, town mayors or chiefs, property owners and their wives (do not forget the anti-Allende March of the Empty Pots by Santiago housewives protesting against food shortages in Chile in 1971) and the professional classes. Tailor your policies to appeal to their own perception of common sense (tinged with a little natural compassion and a rigorously objective administration of justice, where necessary) and their support may be yours. Offend the middle classes at your peril! Unless the working classes are well-organized (i.e., in trades unions), or heavily influenced by demagogues claiming to represent them on public platforms, it is the middle classes that hold the balance of economic power within a country, especially in a peasant economy where the level of participation in national (and even local) politics is uniformly low.

Having said that, however, there are countries where the tone of the national identity is defined and maintained by a small clique right at the top – the aristocracy or royal family (in the cases of, say, Saudi Arabia and Oman) – so their support must be enlisted if the venture is to succeed, unless, of course, they are the very people that you are trying to overthrow. In that case, if the ruling clique is generally unpopular, enlist that power bloc which will do most good most quickly; your selection of such an ally will naturally depend upon your final aims. A socialist revolution in Saudi Arabia could not succeed unless it had a truly Islamic flavour – a Wahhabi Islamic flavour, in fact – so the plotter would have to find some way of enlisting the support of the Wahhabi Muslim majority in Saudi Arabia. However, it is unlikely that a Wahhabi Muslim would embrace any form of socialism – socialism has Communist connotations and it is no coincidence that the term used by many Muslims to describe atheism (which is equally distasteful to them) is a rough translation of the word Muscovite.

Two fairly recent coups d'état that serve to illustrate some of these points are those which placed Albert René in power in the Seychelles in 1977, and General Augusto Pinochet Duarte in power in Chile in 1973. Albert René is a socialist whose own party, the People's United Party, was a junior member of the coalition government formed by President James Mancham after the islands received independence in 1976.

Jimmy Mancham was a 'playboy president' though not in the sense of a 'Baby Doc' Duvalier. He was basically popular, but perhaps his ambitions for the islands were not matched by those of the islanders themselves. On the face of it René could claim a certain justification for overthrowing Mancham while the latter was absent at the Commonwealth Heads of State Conference in London. President Mancham was only too happy to sell parcels of land or whole islands to rich Arabs and socialites, and this worried some people. René made himself popular immediately by re–appropriating the islands (without compensation), introducing wide-reaching social programmes and organizing proper education for all. René's true political complexion began to show only when he instituted a one-party State, censored the newspapers and – in the Seychelles of all places – created an almost 500-strong army.

During the run-up to the presidential elections of 1975, and during earlier campaigns, René's PUP had been suspected of involvement in bombings, intimidation and organized anti-Mancham violence. He was well funded, by Tanzania, many thought, and it was no surprise when Tanzanian troops formed the nucleus of the new Seychelles

Army, described by many as the new President's personal bodyguard. Though perhaps not truly Marxist, the new regime was still not popular and did not become more so as the years passed. It was revolutionary, in Seychelles terms, and has been held responsible for a considerable amount of alleged oppression and even violence. Few Seychellois would have voted for such a regime, but as René was unable to muster sufficient support to achieve his aim by constitutional means, he had to mount a coup d'état.

The failed mercenary counter-coup of 1979, led by Colonel Mike Hoare, was a fairly typical counter–revolutionary coup which, like René's, opened up a new dimension to the coup d'état. Both were organized and executed by mercenaries who came in from offshore. René's surgically precise coup was not the first to be mounted from offshore, however, nor was it the first to succeed. The former Congo mercenary and contemporary of Mike Hoare's, Bob Denard, mounted a successful operation planned along similar lines in The Comoros in 1975, and this undoubtedly led to both René's successful coup and Hoare's ill-fated attempt, on Mancham's behalf, to topple him. These operations and the reasons for their success and failure will be discussed in more detail later on.

The coup which took place in Chile in 1973 was almost inevitable given the moribund nature of Chilean political life and debate at that time, and the misrule (in Chilean eyes) of the Marxist President, Salvador Allende Gossens. For nearly fifty years Chilean political life had become progressively more debased and divorced from the mainstream of public thought, and never more so than under Allende's predecessor, President Frei. Allende was elected in 1970 on a minority vote and, despite signing a Statute of Guarantees which became an amendment to the constitution, proceeded to tinker disastrously with both the economy and the political system. His contacts with the Soviet Union and Cuba grew to alarming proportions. Manipulating the economy in order to seize control of it, he created conditions so unpopular that the bulk of the population united for once in opposing his revolutionary government. The last straw was a combination of national strikes by major union blocs such as the truck drivers, and his reaction to the amateurish coup attempt, the *Tancazo*, which took place in June 1973 and which deserves closer attention.

The economic and political state of Chile had so enraged elements of the army and one particular party, the Patria y Libertad National Front, that a coup was planned jointly by them and officers of the army's 2nd Armoured Regiment, based near Santiago. Military Intelligence discovered the plot, reported it and arrested the officer most heavily implicated. This officer implicated his commanding officer who was relieved of his command forthwith. The 2nd Armoured Regiment went into action almost immediately, leaving its barracks and storming both the Ministry of Defence (where they freed their brother officer) and the Moneda Palace, the presidential headquarters of the Chilean Government. Allende was not there. Hearing of the coup from his home, he immediately went on national radio, appealing for help from 'the workers' and hinting that they would be armed soon. The Army High Command responded to the coup with remarkable speed, dispatching officers to all garrisons in order to keep them under control; the Commander-in-Chief, General Prats, submachine-gun in hand, walked to the Moneda Palace and talked the tank crews, one by one, into surrendering. It was all over by 11.30 on the morning of 29 June, having lasted just three hours.

Allende's reaction had horrified the military, however. The workers had indeed mobilized, but only to seize factories in the name of the government, adding another twist to the spiral of mounting chaos, and this led in part to the army's decision to overthrow Allende. The manner of his overthrow, and his suicide, will be discussed later.

2
OPPORTUNITY
Tides in the Affairs of Men

The very fact that somebody is thinking along the lines of a coup d'état suggests that, in this person's eyes, something is seriously wrong with the country or the government. A coup is a traumatic event in the life of a nation and its consequences may be far-reaching. People do not normally commit themselves to such a course of action unless the motivation to do so is very strong, or unless they are committed revolutionaries of one complexion or another. While a coup is a political act, this is not a political book, so it is not proposed to spend a great deal of time elaborating on some of the theses put forward later. It is enough for our purposes that certain conditions exist which have driven somebody to an unconstitutional (even treasonable) act in order to change and, it is to be hoped, improve those conditions.

In this Chapter we shall discuss a subject around which the coup d'état revolves – the trigger which sets off a train of events resulting in a successful (for the plotters) change of government. A country, or a group of people within a country, can labour for years or generations under burdensome conditions not of its own making, only for a sudden spark to set the edifice of militancy alight and begin a sudden and unforeseen change in the country's or group's circumstances. Even revolutionaries need some sort of trigger (an existing one, or a trigger which they themselves manufacture and squeeze) before a revolutionary coup can be successful.

THE CHILEAN EXPERIENCE

Let us take a few examples. Chile in 1973 is a good place to start because it is today a misunderstood country whose military rulers enjoy greater constitutional legitimacy than a number of so-called 'Democratic' rulers and governments. The bare facts of the case have been mentioned in the previous Chapter, but not the background – President Allende's slim election victory in which he polled only 36.3 per cent of the vote, and only 39,000 votes more than his nearest rival, out of a population of three million people; his written undertaking not to alter or tinker with the Constitution; his disastrous fiscal and industrial policies; his doctrinaire socialism which so upset the people of Chile and brought the country to the verge of ruin. Less well known is the reluctance of the Chilean armed forces to become involved in the political process. Similarly, Allende's attempts to create parallel organizations within Chilean industrial and social life so that he could, in effect, run the country his own way without reference to the senate or to the great mass of the electorate, have remained largely unrecorded.

Chile was (and still is) a country divided; Chilean society and her armed forces, like those of most of her Latin-American neighbours, have traditionally contained a core of extremely conservative people whose sympathies lean towards the right wing. They are balanced by a far greater number of centrists and, for want of a better term, social democrats who feel a greater responsibility towards the administration of social justice in a rapidly developing country. On the far left is the usual core of Marxists, Leninists, Trotskyites and Maoists, found in every country in the world, and whose commitment to revolutionary socialism is matched only by the apathy of the centrists (who are usually social rather than political animals) and the deep suspicion of the conservative right-wing minority.

This pattern is common throughout Latin America, Spain and Italy and, indeed, is simply a more emphatic and polarized version of the social and political divisions encountered in a majority of European countries. Stability in such a country depends very much on the balance between left and right wing and their strengths compared with the silent, uncommitted centre. Once the size of that uncommitted mass begins to diminish in favour of either or both extreme groups, the balance becomes harder to maintain, instability grows in direct proportion to the growing polarization between the two extreme wings, and sooner or later something cracks.

This is what happened in Chile. The left wing came to power with a minority vote, but was well enough organized to be able to use what power it had and to infiltrate almost every part of Chilean life. The results were disastrous and resulted in a rapid diminution of the centrist mass; some deserted to Allende but many more moved to the right. The right-wing backlash which, after so many years of such total misrule, won the support of a majority of the population, was almost inevitable. But what was the trigger for this backlash?

Almost from the day Allende took office in the Moneda Palace, officers in the armed forces became frightened and disgruntled. As the true nature of his government began to show itself, the officers began plotting, though in a desultory fashion. Much of this activity was mere political grumbling, because the officer corps, by and large, was firmly behind the senior generals for whom a coup at that time, was, unthinkable. The visit of the Cuban leader, Fidel Castro, to Santiago in November/December 1971 changed all that. Allende's visit to the Soviet Union, a year later, in order to secure loans which would offset some of the problems he had created for himself, further infuriated the majority of Chileans. Worse, Cubans, Soviets and East Germans were training and arming the really radical left at underground training centres in the provinces. It was becoming clear that, for all his own socialism, Allende was being overtaken rapidly by extremists, far to his own left, over whom he appeared to have no control, though upon whom he relied for support.

On 9 June 1973 the first direct confrontation between armed guerrillas and the security forces occurred at Los Cerrillos airport; the implications of this fire fight left a significant scar on the psyche of the constitutionalists in the armed forces. Intensive arms searches followed all over the country and the scale of the problem was found to be truly awesome. Allende was clearly to blame for encouraging what was, in effect, anarchy and the growth not only of a revolutionary movement, but one which was armed and willing to confront the State directly.

Support for the President, even among the constitutionalists in the armed forces, began to dwindle. Yet back in December 1971 General Pinochet, then the Chief of Staff of the Chilean Army, had declared that coups 'do not occur in Chile', taking the opportunity to strike verbally at a Chilean right-wing newspaper which had criticized the armed forces for supporting Allende. As recently as early 1973, these statements held a ring of truth. The triggers for the coup which overthrew Allende in September 1973 were threefold: an abortive effort which took place less than three weeks after the Los Cerrillos gun battle; secondly, a pronouncement by the country's judiciary that the Allende regime, by virtue of its unconstitutional behaviour, was now illegal under the terms of the national constitution; and thirdly, a suspected plot by the country's left wing to mount a coup of its own in late September 1973, in which the revolution would be taken to its logical but extreme conclusion.

When the plot to overthrow Allende by the Santiago-based 2nd Armoured Regiment was discovered, the coup attempt was, initially, cancelled. An officer implicated in the plot was arrested, however, and he implicated his own Commanding Officer, Lieutenant-Colonel Roberto Souper; the Army's Generals decided to relieve Souper of his command for such insubordination and informed him of their decision. The Generals, now that they had administered military justice – and had been seen to do so – thought that that was an end of the matter. It wasn't! The 2nd Armoured Regiment went into action at 0830 hrs on 29 June.

On hearing of the attempted coup the Army's Commander-in-Chief, General Carlos Prats, telephoned Allende to affirm his own support for the President as did the other service chiefs; Prats then went straight to the NCO's School in Santiago to warn the Commanding Officer to keep his head and to control the men there; Pinochet himself went to the headquarters of the Buin Infantry

Regiment, also in Santiago, to keep the officers and men there under control, while General Oscar Bonilla went to the headquarters of the 2nd Armoured Regiment to talk those troops still there into giving up. Prats, when he had finished at the NCO's School, went straight to the scene of the fighting outside the Moneda Palace and, armed only with a submachine-gun and with no cover against rebel smallarms fire, walked from tank to tank, climbing up on the turrets. By the force of his personality, he persuaded the crews one by one to surrender.

Paradoxically, such constitutional behaviour created as many problems for many of the officers in the armed forces as it solved, though these new problems were of a domestic rather than political nature. Chilean women, 'a feisty lot!', to quote an admiring but wary Argentine of the author's acquaintance, had had enough of Allende and the intolerable burdens his economic policies had placed upon ordinary families. They had demonstrated before, in the so-called March of the Empty Pots, protesting against food shortages. A mistimed announcement by Allende at the beginning of September 1973 that there was only enough bread for three or four more days sealed their contempt for the President and brought their contempt for their menfolk in the armed forces to the surface. Many army and air force wives, amazed that their husbands had not yet overthrown Allende, took to spreading corn at their men's feet – calling them 'chickens'. What effect this had on the *amour propre* of the Chilean officers can only be guessed at, but the flame of militancy had begun to burn just that little bit brighter in the hearts of the armed forces. Machismo, it should be remembered, is not a quality confined solely to Argentina (which claims to have invented the word).

What of Allende? What had he been doing during the *Tancazo*? He had been at home and not at the palace when the coup began, yet despite Prats's telephone call assuring him of the army's loyalty, he went straight to the studios of Radio Corporacion and appealed to the workers: 'I call upon the people to take over the industries, all the firms, to be alert, to pour into the centre of the city, but not to become victims; the people should come out into the streets, but not to be machine-gunned; do it with prudence, using whatever resources may be at hand. If the hour comes, the people will have arms.' In fact, the workers – the Communists and the far-left Central Workers' Confederation – did not come out on the streets; they seized factories instead and, during the next few weeks, created a machine for controlling large areas of the country in addition to the industrial belts.

Allende's betrayal of the loyalty displayed by Prats and his colleagues in the air force and navy cost him his presidency when the armed forces acted in unison to overthrow him. His own blend of socialism, melodrama and sense of theatre cost him his life; he threatened to fight to the end against a coup d'état by the military (or what he considered to be the political right) and, denied a martyr's death in battle when his companions in the Moneda Palace surrendered, he shot himself with the submachine-gun which had been a personal gift from Fidel Castro.

The coups d'état in the Seychelles are poor examples of coups triggered by a particular event or change in circumstances. They were, in the bluntest terms, revolutionary and counter-revolutionary coups with a momentum of their own, requiring no particular trigger save the political ambitions of the men behind them (though even Albert René needed to have some justification in the eyes of the people for what he did). Better examples of different types of trigger are found in the Philippines and Grenada, the former in early 1986 and the latter in 1979 and 1983.

The coup d'état in the Philippines (it was no less than this) was triggered off ostensibly by the presidential elections of January 1986. The incumbent President, Ferdinand Marcos, called a snap election before the end of his term of office, specifically in order to prevent the growing political opposition of Mrs Corazon Aquino from generating enough momentum to defeat him at the polls. A short, intensive campaign followed in which it seemed that the party with the most money would buy the most votes or, rather, buy the most strongmen with whom to cow the electorate into voting for their candidate. Mrs Aquino's campaign (handicapped by the fragmented groupings of her allies) was characterized by promises of electoral rectitude, but these were not enough to offset the huge amounts of money that Marcos paid in bribes and 'sweeteners'. On polling-day itself, electoral malpractice was rife and for once the world's media were on hand to record the blatant intimidation and vote-rigging by which Marcos was able to claim victory.

Marcos had underestimated his opponent. As the widow of an exiled opposition leader, Benigno Aquino, who had been murdered on the steps of the aircraft bringing him back to Manila after a long period of political exile (a murder blamed even now on Marcos and the clique of senior army and air force officers surrounding him), Mrs Aquino had great support among the people who recognized in her the first real focus of opposition to Marcos for some time.

Rigged elections had been a feature of political life in Manila for years, mainly because there had been nobody of sufficient stature to oppose Marcos while uniting the opposition parties. Aquino rallied the fragmented opposition groups, fought Marcos hard, and was then denied the satisfaction of a fair fight. The people, like Aquino herself, were furious. Two of Marcos's lieutenants, the Army Chief of Staff and a former defence minister, seeing which way the wind was blowing, defected to the opposition and barricaded themselves in the Ministry of Defence. The tanks and troops sent by Marcos to winkle them out were confronted by thousands of people who surrounded the building and refused the military access to the ministry. This one small act of defiance by two men – who had ensured that TV camera crews were allowed unlimited access to them within the building – sparked off the chain of events leading to two simultaneous presidential inaugurations – Marcos's and Aquino's – in separate parts of Manila, and the eventual exile to Hawaii of Marcos, his wife and family and several million dollars which he had managed to place abroad against just such a day.

GRENADA – COUP AND COUNTER-COUP

The two coups d'état in Grenada, in March 1979 and October 1983, while revolutionary in complexion and thus not really dependent upon a specific set of circumstances for their momentum, had triggers of their own which were used as justification by their perpetrators. First, the background. During the 1970s political life in Grenada became heavily polarized between two major groups: Maurice Bishop's opposition New Jewel (Joint Endeavour for Welfare, Education and Liberation) Movement, a Marxist-Leninist party, which successfully disguised its true complexion for many years after taking power; and the Grenada United Labour Party (GULP), which was the ruling party headed by Prime Minister Sir Eric Gairy. Gairy, in nearly thirty years' of island politics, had achieved a reputation for corruption which was pretty well unique throughout the Eastern Caribbean and his government seemed to be firmly established; graft and patronage had given him almost personal control over the police and army. In addition, an irregular group of hired thugs, known as the 'Mongoose Gang', became the executive arm of his intimidation machine.

Gairy was universally disliked and feared in Grenada, but as is often the case, the mass of the people were in no position to challenge him constitutionally. Even the Governor-General could do litle to curb Gairy. Thus real opposition was confined to the diametrically opposed New Jewel Movement (NJM) and its leaders, Maurice Bishop and Bernard Coard, who alone seemed to have the guts to stand up to Gairy and to create an organization that was GULP's only real rival and which represented the only alternative at that time to Gairy's all-embracing powers. It is possible that, had Gairy not been so harsh towards any political opposition, the government succeeding his would have been formed by a less radical group – but that is by the way.

Revolutionary thought demands revolutionary action whenever possible. Bishop and Coard spent the years between Independence in 1974 and the early part of 1979 preparing for revolution; a secret military wing of the NJM was created and training was carried out in Guyana and Cuba. Weapons were in short supply but such as were available ended up in safe houses in Grenada or in the outlying islands. An Intelligence-gathering network of quite remarkable efficiency and range was set up and by the end of 1978 the NJM was armed and ready to take power.

Early in 1979 two NJM members were arrested in Washington on charges of smuggling the guns which the NJM had cached on the island. They had been delivered to a senior NJM official, Unison Whiteman; rather than wait for the investigation to name him and place the rest of the NJM at the mercy of Gairy's police, Bishop and Coard went into action. On 12 March 1979 Gairy departed from Grenada to visit Washington; according to the NJM he left orders that the opposition was to be 'rolled up' – the word 'massacre' was used by Bishop – so the NJM seized Grenada on the morning of Tuesday 13 March using Gairy's 'massacre' order as a smokescreen for their real intentions. It is possible that Gairy had ordered a massacre, but this is open to doubt; he was too astute a politician to go out on such a limb. Nevertheless, such was his unpopularity that people were prepared to believe Bishop and to offer him their support. He became the new prime minister and remained so until his death.

The second Grenada coup, in 1983, was far more conventional in that, while revolutionary in complexion, it was triggered off by a confrontation between two ideologues, Maurice Bishop and Bernard Coard, and the prize at stake in this particular power struggle was the survival of the revolution in Grenada, nothing less.

The people of Grenada were completely unaware that they were being ruled by a Marxist-Leninist party, so well had the NJM camouflaged itself. The party could afford to be overtly socialist in outlook without frightening the people; unfortunately the Marxist-Leninist economic theory applied by the NJM does not work and never has done. The Grenadian economy began to falter badly and the people began to blame the NJM. By early 1983 there was a crisis at hand and severe loss of confidence in Bishop's leadership, both among the people and within the NJM. The party (more specifically a small faction led by Bernard Coard and his wife, Phyllis) wanted to take the revolution further – in effect to come 'out of the closet'. Bishop played along, but his heart wasn't in it – he was no cold-blooded theoretician. Finally, in mid-1983 he was forced to accept joint leadership of the party with Coard; the battle for power was on, but Bishop seems to have failed to realize it until too late.

At a number of meetings Bishop was accused by the NJM of being a backslider and, in effect, of 'selling out'. Then a rumour began to spread that the Coards were about to have Bishop assassinated. Events moved fast. A faction of the part-time militia mobilized in order to protect him; they were disarmed and elements of the People's Revolutionary Army (PRA) were alerted. Bishop was denounced at a meeting of the NJM Central Committee and placed under house arrest. The people were enraged by this and, led by Bishop's allies, took to the streets. The Government began to break up, with factions announcing support either for Bishop or 'the Revolution' (in effect, Coard). As unrest grew, a compromise was arrived at by the two men, but it was too late. The people had seen through Coard and identified him as the Marxist-Leninist he was (they still hadn't realized that Bishop was a man of the same political colour). On the morning of 19 October, before the compromise could be announced to the people and Bishop released, a crowd of more than 2,000 had converged on Bishop's house and, carrying him on their shoulders, swept down to Fort Rupert, the administrative headquarters of the PRA. There Bishop set up a provisional headquarters and tried to make contact with both the people of Grenada and the outside world.

This was the signal for Coard to initiate an attack with armoured personnel carriers and élite troops from the PRA (the Fort Rupert garrison had laid down its arms); convinced that he was in a 'make or break' confrontation with Bishop, Coard sent the soldiers in, guns blazing, to disperse the crowd and capture the Prime Minister and his lieutenants. A few minutes after the attack began, a white signal flare rose above Fort Rupert to signify to Coard, waiting at Fort Frederick on the other side of the town, that Bishop and several others had been placed against a wall and shot.

The trigger in this case had been the spontaneous reaction of the Grenadian people to the news of Bishop's house arrest. In fact there had been two coups d'état. The first was a purely political manoeuvre intended to get Bishop out of the Central Committee of the NJM and leave Coard as *de facto* ruler of Grenada; this had been partly successful but was overtaken by events, leading to the second coup at Fort Frederick on 19 October. This coup led in turn to the American Rescue Mission of 25 October 1983 – but that is another story.

It is vitally important, while considering these examples, to bear in mind what Shakespeare describes as the 'tide in the affairs of men'. Circumstances can conspire to create a perfect opportunity for the quick-witted and well-organized to seize power with, at the very least, no organized opposition and, with luck, a certain amount of popular support.

One thing which nearly every coup has in common is the suggestion, if not the promise, of better times ahead. It will be clear from what has been said that if a coup is to succeed a moral case must be presented which the people who matter – the People themselves – will accept. In the absence of overwhelming force it is their consent which makes or breaks a government in the end, and the coup plotter's best friend is a perceptible withdrawal of that consent by the people from the incumbent government.

Let us take another example – a fictitious example, this time. It is almost inconceivable that a coup d'état could be mounted in the United Kingdom at present. For all that Britain in the 1980s is a divided nation with serious social problems, the basic structure of British society and social life remains intact. That miracle of consensus and common sense, the British Constitution (which is not a constitution at all, in any formal sense) has evolved over the years to create a political system which, if imperfect, offers the electorate the expectation of a change in government whenever they really want one. What if this expectation, this safety-valve, were to be denied the people?

Let us suppose that an extremist party came to power on a manifesto which included the abolition of the Upper Chamber in Britain's bicameral parliamentary system, the House of Lords. Many would fail to grasp the significance of such a move. The House of Lords is a consultative body with no direct powers over the House of

Commons, to which members of parliament must be elected every five years; the only power the Lords have is to veto any extension of the five-year term of office. Remove this power of veto and any party with a large enough majority in the Commons could vote itself an indefinite term of office.

In such a situation, where the constitution was being manipulated by political cynics, an unpopular government could not be removed from office by a general election because there simply wouldn't be one; the best that the electorate could hope for would be a series of by-elections through which the number of opposition members of parliament could be increased gradually until they were in a majority; even then, the Prime Minister would not be obliged to call a general election! If the government became unpopular enough, the conditions could exist for a coup d'état to take place in the United Kingdom, one which (if intelligently run) would remove the ruling party and, it is to be hoped, restore the British Constitution without affecting the Monarch whose constitutional role lies outside party politics and direct involvement in government. Political violence is anathema to most Britons, but so also is 'unsportsmanlike behaviour'. A coup d'état carried out by the right people and presented to the population in the right way could enjoy tremendous support.

The 'Generals' coup' in Algeria in 1961 is another example of circumstances conspiring to create conditions in which a coup could be mounted, though it must be said that this particular one was doomed to failure from the outset. The conditions were these: Algeria was at the time a part of Metropolitan France and was heavily populated by people from the mainland or their descendants – the 'pieds noirs'. The Algerians themselves were looking towards independence, and a number of militant guerrilla and terrorist organizations were formed to achieve this end. The French Army, including the Foreign Legion, whose depot and spiritual home was in the Algerian city of Sidi-bel-Abbès, fought a long, brutal and very nearly successful counter-insurgency campaign against these guerillas, in the belief that they were defending their homeland.

In 1960 the Algerian war had become too much for the French Government and President De Gaulle prepared to meet the guerrillas in order to talk about the possibility (it was no more than that) of Algerian independence. Four French Generals conspired together, urged on by a number of more junior officers (many of them heavily politicized members of the 1st Foreign Parachute Regiment, ler REP); on 21 April they struck and Les Paras (Army as well as Foreign Legion) took over Algiers and other centres in Algeria. The pieds noirs, delirious with joy at this development, hit the streets of Algiers, chanting and blowing their car horns in the five-note cadence *Al-gé-rie Fran-çaise*, repeated over and over again.

A constitutional crisis of enormous proportions had been visited upon the French Government, but, for reasons we shall examine later, the coup was a complete failure – the Generals' rule lasted only five days and ended in imprisonment or a miserable life on the run for most of them. One reason for its failure (there were many, but only two or three were really important) was that the Government of Algeria was that of France herself – and was situated in Paris. The coup could not succeed without Paris itself being taken. Another important reason for its failure was that, although the pieds noirs supported it, many in mainland France did not – the French people were sick of this brutal, unrelenting war which had claimed so many of their sons and which was such a drain on the nation's resources. The people of France, like the conscript soldiers, whose apathy and indifference kept them out of the coup, simply didn't care about Algeria. They cared enough about France, however, to prove to the coup's leader, General Challe, that he could never succeed, and so he surrendered.

The examples of triggers cited so far are spectacular ones, highly visible pegs upon which coup plotters and the general public were able to hang a sense of grievance. Often, however, such pegs are not so prominent and the people are consequently so much less concerned about conditions that they have not even thought about taking sides in a power struggle or about the possibility of modifying the status quo.

It was stated earlier that revolutionary and counter-revolutionary coups have a momentum of their own and do not really need a trigger as such. This is quite true, but it must be remembered that the existence of a revolutionary movement within a country suggests a basic dissatisfaction with existing conditions. This dissatisfaction may not be shared by many people and the revolutionary movement may have little chance of gaining power and putting the revolution into practice. If, however, the revolutionaries can find a peg upon which to hang their coup, one with which the people can identify, the possibility of a coup being successful is greatly increased.

Let us look again at Grenada. The 1979 coup succeeded because the existing government was so unpopular that anything was considered to be better. By camouflaging their true political complexion so successfully, the leaders of the NJM were able to seize power on a wave of popular support – and even to win the qualified support of ordinary people in other Eastern Caribbean countries (though not, for a variety of reasons, their governments). It is possible that the governments knew more about the NJM than they wished to say publicly. Even Sir Eric Gairy's wife, Cynthia, went of her own accord to Radio Grenada to appeal to Grenadians not to resist (and presumably get hurt or killed), but to stay calm and support Bishop. The newly appointed Governor-General of Grenada, Sir Paul Scoon, took no part in the proceedings, but was presumably responsible, directly or indirectly, through a studied silence on his own part, for the decision of Her Majesty's Government in London not to accede to St Lucia's request for British troops and the Royal Navy's Caribbean guard ship to intervene in Grenada, as had happened in 1969 in Anguilla.

The 1983 coup d'état in Grenada was a failure. True, it succeeded in placing Bernard Coard in power and gave him a stranglehold on the island, but he had alienated both the population and Sir Paul Scoon so much that desperate appeals for help went out to Britain and the United States, both from Grenada and the Organization of Eastern Caribbean States (OECS). The rest, as they say, is history; the Americans (but not, strangely, the British) responded with massive force and succeeded in ousting Coard's government. For the time being Grenada's still-fragile new democracy is sponsored by the United States.

Another revolutionary coup which needed a peg upon which it could be hung to the public's satisfaction was Albert René's, in the Seychelles in 1977. His predecessor, Jimmy Mancham, was basically popular but perhaps a little too big for his boots, especially in a close-knit island community. The question of selling off land and whole islands to foreigners had enraged enough people for René to make this one of the corner-stones of his later justification for the coup. He was convincing enough, and the whole issue was emotive enough to the Seychellois, for René to be assured of instant (though short-lived) popularity. Once in power, of course, he had no further need of popular support and the revolution could begin.

A non-revolutionary coup which, nevertheless, achieved widespread support was the New Year's Eve 1983 coup d'état which placed the military back in power in Nigeria. In August 1985, however, the man who was made figurehead of the new military government, Major-General Muhammadu Buhari, was overthrown by one of his co-triumvirs from the three-man junta which was effectively governing Nigeria. Buhari's economic programme had done little for the country, and his administration of justice for those convicted of corruption was just a little too hard. Besides, he had allowed another of the 'big three', Major-General Tunde Idiagbon, too free a hand in running the National Security Organization, to the detriment of morale in government and the armed forces but, one suspects, the betterment of Idiagbon's financial affairs (though this last charge, it must be said, has not been proven). The third member of the ruling triumvirate, Major-General Ibrahim Babangida, waited until Idiagbon was in Mecca during the annual Muslim hadj and then, with the head of the NSO out of the way, mounted a neat little bloodless coup which displaced Buhari, gave Babangida the title of President (the first time, incidentally, that a Nigerian military head of state had ever taken this title) and afforded him a brief honeymoon in which to try to win the confidence of the Nigerian people.

In January 1986, however, Babangida came close to losing both his Presidency and his life when a clique of highly politicized army and air force officers, angered both by his economic policies and his rejection (following a national plebiscite on the subject, which gave him his mandate) of a deal with the International Monetary Fund (IMF), planned to overthrow the government in a particularly bloody and violent coup. It is probably indicative both of Nigeria's basic acceptance of Babangida at the time, and the loyalty he commanded within the armed forces, that this plot was discovered by the security services and reported to him. After all, other coups have been planned and mounted in Nigeria without the doomed heads of state knowing anything about them until they found themselves in prison or in their graves. It is probably fair to say that the January 1986 plot, even if successful in military terms, would not have produced a long-lasting government – neither the people nor the armed forces would have wanted much to do with the new government.

SPARE PEGS

If we look around we can see other pegs upon which coups d'état may be hung with rather more success than the 1986 plot in Nigeria. The Latin-American debt crisis, and the response both of the IMF and individual nations to the economic problems it has caused in South America, is just such a peg. All it might take is a controversial statemeht by either a government or some external agency which might be seen to have a disproportionate influence on the country's affairs, and a trigger could exist.

Similarly, the fall in world oil prices has led to severe hardship for, among others, Nigeria, Venezuela, Mexico, some of the Gulf States and a number of countries in the Far East. Any suggestion that economic mismanagement has led to an unnecessary harshening of conditions could equally be the peg upon which some plotter hangs his coup. The Middle East is rife with internecine quarrels, some revolving around Israel, some around the Gulf War, some around relations with America and some around doctrinal questions that concern the very nature of Islam. If, for example, Israel were to attack Jordan (which is so unlikely as to be out of the question, so this must of necessity be a fictitious example), any Arab head of state who did not immediately express support for Jordan, and then back his words with some show of force, would be extremely vulnerable to the backlash which his inaction would generate, not only among the militants but among the general population.

Israel makes an interesting study in itself, however. The country is divided politically between the right-wing Likud coalition and the basically social-democrat Herut (Labour) coalition. If some of the more extremist members of Likud were to rise to power, and then start a social or political programme designed to inflame the Arabs beyond all caution and cause the rest of Israel to worry for the country's future safety as a result (and this is not fanciful speculation – militant clerics and politicians could do just this, given half a chance), a coup d'état by a coalition of moderate politicians and senior officers in the armed forces would, in the opinion of many, be almost inevitable. This would have the dual benefits of placating the Arabs and, for a while at least, imposing a single, unified government over Israel which would not be racked by the political infighting and shabby compromise which have created so many economic problems there in the past.

Similarly, South Africa has been ripe for a coup d'état by some faction or other since the early 1980s, but more especially since the rise of extremely hardline Afrikaner-dominated groups on the right wing of South African politics. Two scenarios come to mind: first, the increasing liberalization of the South African government, leading to fears among the old guard of the political right that a sellout is under way. This could provoke a coup d'état by the right-wing militants, backed up by those Commando and Citizen Force members in and around Pretoria, Cape Town, Johannesburg, Durban and other major centres, who believe that liberalism has gone too far. Alternatively, the imposition of sanctions on South Africa by the rest of the world could result in increased violence in the townships; tribal divisions among the blacks (and one looks in vain for real unity among South

Africa's blacks) would probably lead to some sort of blacks-only civil war between moderates and militants.

Remember that sanctions would have an immediate and painful effect on the blacks and a far slower effect on the whites – for this reason alone the moderates are likely to be less than pleased at the success of the militants in getting sanctions imposed. Increasing violence would lead inevitably to sterner law enforcement by the South African police and an army growing increasingly weary of a role for which it wasn't raised and which is doing its reputation no good. This could lead to fears among the moderates that a 'win or die' confrontation with the blacks was in the offing, a confrontation which the whites would not win; and so a coup d'état by moderate whites, backed up by the armed forces (who have a realistic appreciation of their own capabilities against an overwhelming level of civil disobedience and terrorism by the blacks), could occur.

West Germany could conceivably undergo a coup d'état. If, for example, the Green Party were to take power and decide to throw all foreign troops and nuclear weapons out of the country, the prospect of NATO's wholesale dismemberment by a politically naïve government would probably result in a coup of some sort by West German centrists and conservatives (possibly assisted by other NATO members) in order to maintain a semblance of unity in what would by then be a very troubled alliance indeed. The problem with such a coup would be that it could be interpreted by the Warsaw Pact as a right-wing backlash with sinister neo-Nazi overtones, and the frightening (to them) prospect in the long term of a reunited Germany. The effect this would have on international relations across the Inner German Border can only be guessed at. The prognosis, however, would not be good.

There are any number of political issues which can be exploited by a plotter to the greater advantage of the coup, but the trick is to find one that not only unites the country in criticism of the government, but is serious enough to justify some kind of direct action to which the people can relate. Every country has its own set of problems which can be interpreted or presented as justification for the overthrow of the government, and any astute politician on the ground will spot these opportunities for himself.

What if the right sort of opportunity doesn't exist, however? What if the constitution works properly, the government has a firm grasp on political power and the people are basically happy (or not too unhappy) with them? The plotter had best beware; the electorate is not so stupid that it will swallow unreservedly any doctrinaire apologia for a coup d'état. Lame excuses cannot be dressed up to look like strong moral or political arguments.

It is possible to create an issue worthy of a coup d'état, but this needs time and some very slick propaganda. The accepted technique is to find some dormant issue which may have fundamental importance within the country, but which has never created a problem before; while the majority of people and the government itself are happy with the status quo there is little chance of it erupting. If, however, the issue can be tied to some weakness or failing on the part of the government, a crisis can be conjured up almost from thin air, especially if the *modus operandi* of the government is disreputable (or just plain ambiguous) enough to catch the eye of both opposition and media. It helps also if the media are not muzzled by the government in any way. Even if they are, it may be possible to make political capital out of the issue by seeming to be forced to use 'underground' means such as posters, handbills and demonstrations, to open the public's eyes.

Once a political confrontation is under way, the government could react in one of two ways, depending on the rightness of its cause and the respect it has for free speech. It could become embarrassed and defensive (thereby admitting a measure of responsibility for the situation), or it could go over to the offensive and create a climate of distrust and suspicion simply by stifling debate on the subject. Astute politicians do this sort of thing all the time, using any material that comes to hand to embarrass the opposition: it could be a national debate about abortion, or over armed forces' pay, immigration, political alliances or almost anything at all. Every government has something to hide and most are easily embarrassed. If this capacity for embarrassment can be harnessed to the right sort of issue, anything can happen.

Of course, such a campaign might result in power changing hands constitutionally at the next election. Much will depend on the strength of the country's political institutions; the weaker they are the more scope there is for somebody to manipulate them so as to remain in power, and the greater acceptance (or more accurately, the less resentment) there is likely to be of a coup d'état. Remember that weak political institutions receive very little respect from either government or electorate. The latter will almost certainly suspect the government of manipulating or 'bending' them in some way; the politicians will probably do exactly that in any case. Chile in 1973 is a case in point, except that a major constitutional crisis was in progress which gave the coup plotters their mandate. Pakistan is another. Notwithstanding the bad publicity the military regime of General Zia ul-Haq has received, some of the politicians in Pakistan deserve no better for the way in which they made a mockery of constitutional behaviour, especially in the run-up to a previous coup d'état in 1958.

The 1958 coup makes an interesting study. The key to it all was a murder which took place in the East Bengal Parliament (East Bengal is now part of Bangladesh). The Opposition managed to get the Speaker certified as insane, thus allowing the Deputy Speaker, their own man, to take over in order, it is alleged, to 'fudge' an election in the Opposition's favour. Government supporters in Parliament went berserk at the next session and beat the unfortunate Deputy Speaker to death. The politicians had long been considered by the Pakistani people to be a waste of time; they compared badly with the incorruptibility and efficiency of an army moulded in the British tradition. In the wake of the East Bengal Parliament fracas the army gave the President little choice (if he wanted to maintain any confidence in the Government) other than to dissolve Parliament, dissolve the political parties and declare martial law with General Ayub Khan as its chief administrator. Two weeks later he appointed the General as Prime Minister and, four days after this, handed over all power to him and resigned.

Similarities between Pakistan in 1958 and Chile in 1973 are interesting; the military in both countries were traditionally reluctant to soil their hands with politics and it was only with some reluctance (in their faces, at any rate, but who knows how much alacrity in their hearts?) that they accepted the political power fate seemed to have thrust upon them.

Of course, the method whereby an issue is made out of some real or imagined deficiency in the way the government is doing its job must be considered carefully; there would be little sense in an opposition politician behaving with a sudden piety and nobility that was quite out of character – most politicians are considered to be hypocrites in any case, so there is little point in singling oneself out for special treatment. This would only arouse the suspicion of the Press, public and government itself, and might give rise to pardonable cynicism on the part of a public confronted with apparently noble motives for mounting a coup d'état.

To summarize this Chapter: coups d'état do not happen spontaneously; they arise from the conjunction of Motive and Opportunity, fuelled by desire and carried through using the necessary Means. Desire is initiated by a trigger or it may arise from revolutionary motives that require only a peg – an Opportunity – on which to hang the sense of grievance used to justify the coup.

As we are discussing an essentially political problem, which is outside the main scope of this book, this is probably a good point at which to leave the politically minded reader to carry on with his or her own research into specific cases, extrapolating from what has been said here. The next Chapters follow logically from this one; once it has been decided that a coup d'état is desirable (from the point of view of the plotters), it remains to be seen whether it is feasible. We shall consider the *Means* by which power can be transferred from the hands of the government into the hands of the plotters or their nominees.

3
MEANS
Suiting the Means to the End

The coup d'état is a means to an end. The execution of the coup must be so planned that what is won is exactly what is required, no more and no less. Thus, while power is the end to which the plotter is working, he must consider carefully the nature of the power he wishes to assume and plan his coup accordingly. It is not enough simply to incarcerate the Establishment and run the country in their place; in most countries this would be physically impossible so the planning must take into account the level of involvement in government desired by the principals to the coup – those people, whose identities are outlined in the preceding Chapter, who might be important allies in the post-coup climate and whose friendship must not be compromised.

When considering the exact nature of what one is trying to achieve, one gets some idea of the means needed to secure that achievement – and we can forget immediately the old cliché, *the end justifies the means.* This simply is not true. Very few successful coup plotters are fortunate enough to be so powerful that they can ignore the consequences of what they have done. Absolute power takes so long to emerge that a reckless, highly unpopular takeover leaves the plotters vulnerable to the anger of the masses for some time to come. The object of the coup, remember, is not only to seize power but to hold it for as long as is required. The means, therefore, must be appropriate to the end.

In considering the means it is vital to start at the very beginning and identify the immediate targets of the coup in terms of the institutions and agencies that must be either controlled or suborned in order to effect your seizure of power. On the face of it, a simple seizure of the presidential palace will suffice, but the truth is that real power in any country lies in the hands not only of government, but of agencies and individuals outside formal governmental circles, whose ability to apply pressure or sanctions of one kind or another affects government policy and the decision-making process. The chances are that they are in a position to influence the post-coup government, possibly to an unacceptable degree, so they must be either neutralized or suborned.

Another point to bear in mind is the strength (or otherwise) of existing alliances with foreign countries. A country enjoying particularly strong ties with, say, the United States or the Soviet Union, might be said to be sponsored by that power – at any rate, its government may be sponsored – so that any move to overthrow the government must bear in mind the likely reaction of its sponsors. Any move today to reimpose a revolutionary government in Grenada, for example, would almost certainly meet with a military response. Similarly, a coup d'état in Czechoslovakia by a less rigidly Communist government would simply provoke 'fraternal assistance to a socialist state' of the kind we saw in 1968.

Similarly, a major industrial group that wields disproportionate economic power may be in a position to make or break a government by either offering or withdrawing its support. Such was the case with the huge Union Minière group in Southern Zaïre during the early 1960s; the Union Minière not only could but did pay for mercenaries to come and fight its corner. In modern times a small country like St Lucia in the Eastern Caribbean could become a hostage to its one-crop economy. If the purchasing commodities group decided not to send its boats to the island's capital, Castries, to pick up the bananas which are the major export commodity of most Eastern Caribbean states, and if it could persuade other companies to boycott the island, disaster – political disaster, if nothing else – would follow.

CHOOSING THE TARGETS

Internally, there are similar factors to be considered – one of the most important being the identification of the real source of political power within the country. In Israel, for example, the most powerful man in the country is probably the Prime Minister, Minister of Defence or the Foreign Minister, not the President. Similarly, in the United Kingdom one does not look to the Monarch to make political decisions, one looks to the Prime Minister and the cabinet. In France, however, or in the United States, one would have to eliminate the President as part of the coup plan because he holds real executive power. In America one would have also to secure the other two bastions of power – the senate and the judiciary. Being a federal organization, one could neutralize the judiciary at the same time as the President, because they are both located in Washington, DC. The senate is another problem entirely – or, rather, the states the senators represent are the problem. Like West Germany, the United States of America is exactly what its name implies – a federation of states enjoying considerable devolved powers of self-government. To keep the states united after a coup, it would be necessary to enlist the support of the senators, the people they represent and the state governors. No easy task, that.

A country where the head of state has executive power thus poses something of a problem; not only is it necessary to govern the country, but to maintain its unity and the unanimity of national support for the institution of government. A country whose head of state has ceremonial or only minor constitutional powers may be much easier to keep united, especially if the head of state has as high a profile as the Queen in the United Kingdom and commands as much respect and affection. A coup d'état which left the monarchy intact and (unlikely as it might seem) enjoyed some sort of tacit support or approval from Her Majesty might succeed in both seizing power and enjoying the support of the nation.

What other agencies or institutions must be secured? Potentially every cabinet minister, under-secretary and junior minister must be either suborned or neutralized. Senior civil servants, whose example might turn the civil service as a whole against the new government, must be dealt with in a similar way. The senior military figures (Chief of the Defence Staff, Joint Chiefs of Staff and so on), if they are not part of the plot, must not be allowed to hinder it. If they are likely to be hostile to the idea (and there have been plenty of examples of this) they must be neutralized also.

Political parties have no shortage of personalities who enjoy little formal status or power but whose counsels carry a great deal of weight with their peers and their superiors. They, and senior party officials outside government who might be able to rally support against the plot, must be considered as potential targets. In many cases they will acquiesce with the *fait accompli* the coup, it is to be hoped, will represent, but politics attracts its own fair share of principled men and women, many of whom do not mind the prospect of becoming martyrs, and they must be watched carefully.

So much for 'the Government'; what about the rest of 'the Establishment'? Which organizations within the state are well enough organized, unanimous in their outlook and sufficiently militant under the right circumstances to be mobilized by a call to action from oppnents of the coup?

Trades unions are almost universally well organized – this is the basis of their power. Also, it is in their nature to be large, monolithic bodies controlled from the top or from regional centres by small groups of committed men and women who are elected to positions of authority by members who are, in the main, not very interested in the political struggles which their leaders are often engaged in. So, potentially or actually hostile trades union leaders must be neutralized – fortunately there tend not to be too many of them, considering the power they wield in the form of organized manpower.

Industrial conglomerates, for all their undoubted economic power, tend to be apolitical. Captains of industry, confronted by a coup, will tend to adopt a cautious, 'wait and see' attitude to what happens, and try to make the best out of it later on. Their power to cripple an economy by withdrawing funds from the country and shutting down their various operations is not to be ignored, but does not represent an immediate threat. Only if the new government is particularly unpleasant and stupid in its financial dealings will industry either bale out or fight back. The former is more likely in the case of a foreign firm, the latter in that of a local one.

What about the students, those ever-idealistic pawns of rabble-rousers down the centuries? Students are not usually as militant as the Press makes out, unless they feel their own prospects and interests are threatened. The right sort of approach can ensure their virtual acquiescence, especially if the new government looks like being a worthwhile one. Students, like trades union members, are easily led, however; this is a function of the fact that they are organized and enjoy a certain *espirit de corps* arising from their common status. Student leaders, like trades union leaders, do not always reflect the real thinking of their constituency so it is important to decide whether the power they have over their fellows can be used in one's own favour or not. A left-wing coup in a country with left-wing dominated unions and students would benefit from the assistance of their militant leaders; a coup by the right wing or the centrists might have a better chance of success if the student leaders have been neutralized.

What about the opposition parties, if there are any? It is possible, of course, that the coup is being organized by the opposition in the first place, but if it is not, how can they be either enlisted or neutralized? Neutralization is easy; the party leaders should be dealt with in the same way as government party leaders. Enlistment may be problematical. One of the problems with opposition parties is that their hunger for power may not match their respect for constitutional behaviour. Also, they may feel uncomfortable in being associated with the coup plotters; there is no guarantee that their political programmes will survive the partnership with the plotters, still less that they will be allowed a free hand to do as they wish. In any case, a party that has been put into power by a coup can just as easily be removed. If the opposition prefers not to be associated with the coup, so be it. If they won't help, they must not be allowed to hinder.

Who else must be considered? Devolved power sources such as local governments and state or province assemblies, especially if they are dominated by people hostile to the coup, must be neutralized. In a sense, dealing with these people will be no different from dealing with national government, but there is one difference: a local politician may be much better known to his constituents than a member of the national assembly. Maltreat this person and his many friends and family may mobilize local opinion against the plot. Do it often enough and you have an entire province – soon the entire nation – up in arms.

Finally, what about the armed forces? It has been implicit so far that it is they who are mounting the coup, but this is not necessarily the case. Of all the services it is most likely that the army will plan and mount the coup; for one thing, the army usually boasts the greatest manpower, not to mention the equipment and weapons necessary for subduing a capital city. Secondly, a small air force or navy is in no position to do much more than lend moral support, by virtue of the fact that their equipment may be based some distance from the centres of power and, in any case, is more suited to mass destruction than surgical precision. However, the unity of the armed forces must not be destroyed if at all possible. If indeed it is the army that is taking power, the two other services must share some of the perquisites and responsibilities of government otherwise the unity and defence of the realm become, to put it mildly, major problems.

A much happier situation is total unanimity between all three services, and this is frequently the case. If the coup is planned at the right level of command, liaison between the services can be excellent and ensure that the army has a free hand to do what it likes, secure in the knowledge that it doesn't have to worry about airfields, airports, docks and waterways. Indeed, marines and air force ground troops may be only too happy to assist in securing the capital or other regional centres. If the worst comes to the worst, the threat of a naval or aerial bombardment has been known to have an electrifying effect on the incumbent head of state.

The problem of enlisting support from among the nation's armed forces will be addressed in more detail later on. Let us consider, though, one fairly recent phenomenon which has altered the way in which coups d'état are mounted – mercenaries.

To the author's knowledge there have been eight coups planned in recent times which would have involved the use of mercenaries or irregular troops rather than government troops. Bob Denard has mounted three, two of them successful: in The Comoros in 1975 and again in 1978 (coup and counter-coup organized by the same man – very bad form!); his unsuccessful attempt was the abortive airborne assault on Cotonou, Benin, in 1977. Two coups d'état took place in the Seychelles: one, successful, in 1977 and Mike Hoare's unsuccessful attempt in 1981; earlier, in 1979, Maurice Bishop had taken over Grenada in a coup mounted by men coming in from one of the outlying islands; and there are reports that a mercenary coup was attempted in the Seychelles in 1979. Finally, a boatload of mercenaries en route from Brazil to Ghana was apprehended early in 1986 amid allegations that they were on their way to overthrow the military government of Flight-Lieutenant Jerry Rawlings. Few details of this operation have been released.

It is rumoured (though not proven) that Frederick Forsyth, best-selling author of *The Dogs of War*, based his novel on an unsuccessful plot, which he hatched, to take over the West African island state of Fernando Po (part of the Republic of Equatorial Guinea) in 1973. The book centres on the attempt by a small group of mercenaries to make an amphibious landing on a fictitious state's coastline, close to the capital, and destroy all resistance as well as the head of state in one night. By dawn, the white mercenaries would be out of sight and a new government with black troops trained by the mercenaries would be in power.

Forsyth has denied the rumours and there is no published evidence to suggest that they are true. Perhaps the people of Fernando Po wish they were, and that Forsyth's alleged coup had succeeded, for the then-ruler of Fernando Po and Equatorial Guinea was every bit as

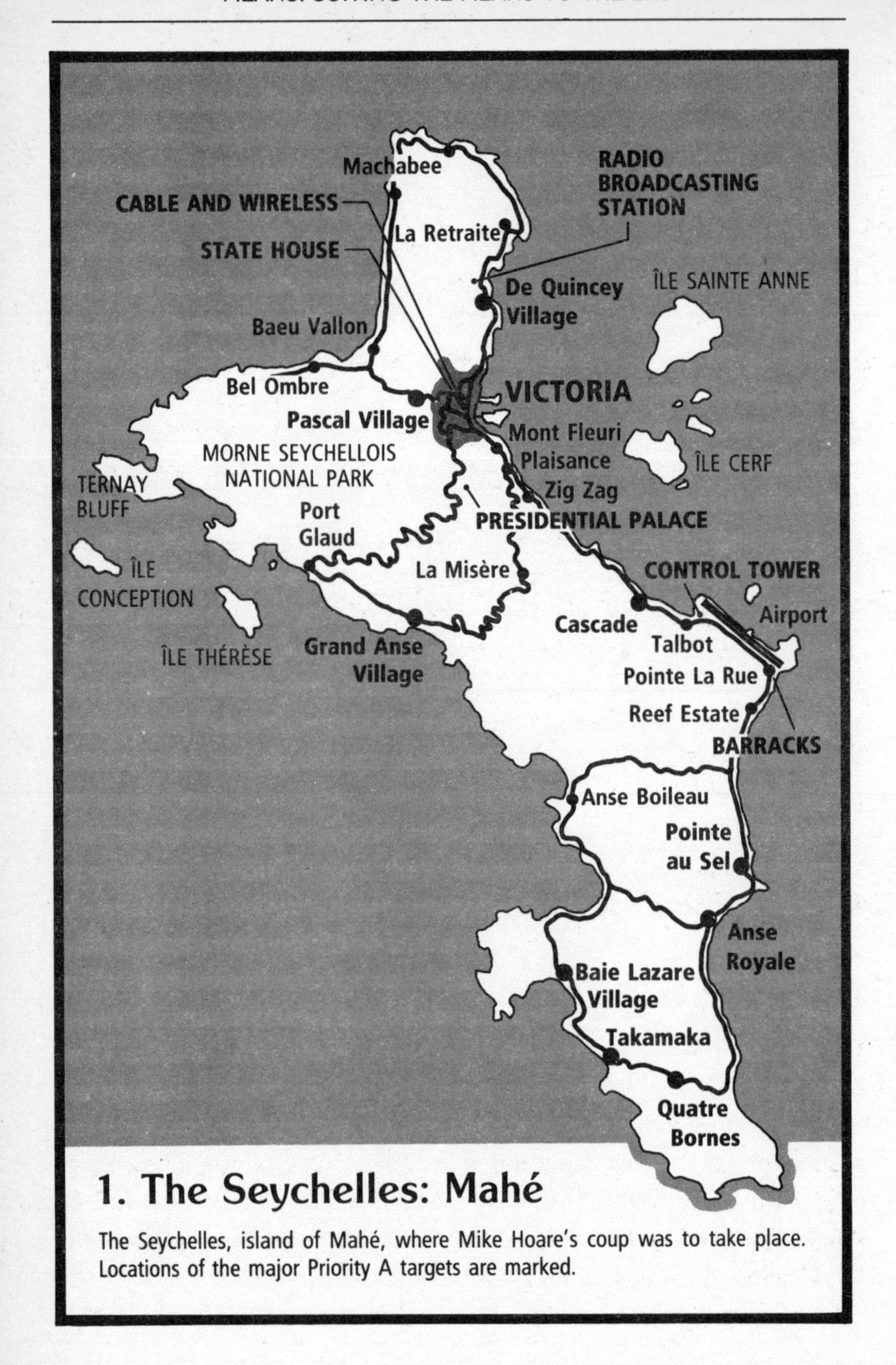

1. The Seychelles: Mahé

The Seychelles, island of Mahé, where Mike Hoare's coup was to take place. Locations of the major Priority A targets are marked.

nasty as the fictional head of state whom Forsyth's fictional characters wipe out.

The use of mercenaries in this way, then, is a new development, but not one that has ever been used in a large or developed country. In each of the eight cases mentioned, the mercenaries came in from well outside the national frontiers, either by air or sea, and mostly had very little material support in-country. Their role was confined simply to assaulting specified, fixed targets such as the presidential palace, police and army barracks, radio stations and armouries. Their tasks were completed as soon as these targets were secure and the new government had proclaimed its seizure of power. In only a few instances did any of the mercenaries remain to spend the money they had been paid.

What made mercenary operations feasible in these cases was the fact that each of the countries concerned was small and undeveloped, often with no armed forces to speak of. By 'taking out' the president and one or two key points, as outlined in Forsyth's book, it was possible to seize power almost in a matter of minutes using a small force and maximum surprise. Such a technique wouldn't work elsewhere – in Nigeria, for example – with a more developed economy, national infrastructure and political awareness among the population. Nevertheless, it is instructive to look at some of these coups as illustrations, on a small scale, of how a coup d'état works on the larger scale. Some of the lessons will be discussed later.

SCALE MODEL

One of the best examples is the failed Seychelles coup mounted by Colonel Michael 'Mad Mike' Hoare in November 1981. The failure of this coup is no reflection on Hoare's bold and imaginative planning, and it is the planning with which we are most interested. The targets for his 54-man mercenary unit were, in order of importance: the radio station and main army barracks (in which Seychellois and Tanzanian troops, the former in the majority, were housed); State House; army headquarters and another barracks, these last three all lying within the capital city, Victoria. D-Day was planned for Friday 27 November, at about midday. A cabinet meeting would be in progress at State House although President René would be out of the country at the time.

Simultaneously with the attack on State House a second assault would go in against the radio station, just one mile to the north. While a third assault went in against the main army barracks at Pointe La Rue, next to the airport and about six miles to the south, the group in the radio station using a pre-recorded message would announce the overthrow of René, then another tape made by Jimmy Mancham, the ex-president, would announce that he was back in the Seychelles and resuming his presidential post. In fact, he would be in Kenya, waiting for a radio message to tell him that the airport was secure and that it was safe for him to fly in.

Hoare would establish his own base at the Cable & Wireless offices in Victoria to ensure that the Seychelles were cut off from anyone he himself did not wish to contact; the implication, of course, is that René or his deputies could contact Tanzania and ask for troops to be flown in to overcome the plotters. All in all it was a good plan and carried also the seal of approval of two other governments, both alarmed at the growth of revolutionary socialism in the Indian Ocean, South Africa and Kenya. Many of Hoare's mercenaries were South African part-time troops, members of the South African Defence Force's 'Citizen Force'. The weapons used, AK-47 assault rifles, had been captured in Angola and issued to Hoare by the South African Government, and one of Hoare's planners was a member of the South African secret service. The Kenya connection simply allowed Mancham a base from where he could await developments and then fly in when ordered. Help of a more concrete kind was available if required, however: once Mancham was established, Kenyan troops would be available to fly in as soon as requested by the new government.

Two other factors made a huge amount of difference: local support for the coup was virtually guaranteed; and the local underground opposition, *Mouvement pour la Résistance*, would be taking over some of the more mundane duties of the mercenaries, such as guarding prisoners and the radio station itself, while Hoare's men were occupied with consolidating the situation.

Given that the Seychelles were (and are) an underdeveloped area with little infrastructure and diminutive political and governmental establishments, what lessons are there to be learned from 'Mad Mike's' plan? The first is *speed* – leave no time for the loyalists to react. The second is *isolation* – seize all means of mass communication (the media) and operational communications (military radios, telephone exchanges) in order to isolate the various elements of potential resistance. The third is *targeting* – select the immediate human targets of the coup for their ability to offer resistance of any kind, and remove them either in order of importance or, preferably, simultaneously. The fourth lesson is *timing* – carry out these operations at once if possible and at a time when as many of your targets are as accessible as possible. The fifth and final lesson is *Intelligence* – knowing who, what and where the targets are, what their strength is and how they may be 'taken out' with the minimum of effort.

These five features of the classical coup d'état were all present in Hoare's plan. For reasons we shall discover later (see 'Execution') the plan was never allowed the chance to succeed, but there is no doubt in the minds of many that it would have done. Returning, however, to the earlier part of this Chapter, what else have we learned about the means necessary for seizure of power?

First of all, there must be sufficient strength available to make seizure of the major targets a *fait accompli.* Secondly, communications and organization must be good enough for the entire coup to be carried out in a single operation, but one encompassing many diverse elements. Thirdly, any opposition must be fragmented and must remain so without any opportunity to regroup or appeal directly to the masses for support. Fourthly, the mass electronic media must be in the plotter's own hands at an early stage so that the population is told only what the plotters want it to hear. Presenting the people with what seems to be a *fait accompli*, even if there are pockets of resistance and parts of the operation look marginal, may tip the scales in one's own favour, especially if (as often happens) the loyalists are themselves listening to the radio or watching television.

For the immediate purposes of our coup, then, what are our aims? Much will depend, naturally, on our knowledge of the head of state's whereabouts. If he or she is out of the country at the time, so much the better. If not, the head of state is the first target. The aim, therefore, must be simultaneously to seize the head of state and as many of his most powerful and loyal lieutenants as possible; physically secure the presidential palace and as many ministries as possible; seize the major radio and TV stations, seize and shut down temporarily major communications centres such as international telex and telephone stations; close down air and sea ports (these last two in order to prevent the flight of capital from a country one will be ruling very soon); and seal off that area of the capital in which the business of government is concentrated.

Once these primary targets are secure the plotters have comparative leisure in which to carry out the secondary tasks such as rounding up trades union officials and potentially hostile political personalities. It cannot be emphasized too strongly how important it is to monopolize the mass media. It is rarely appreciated, even now, how much any population's mind is made up by 'talking heads' or disembodied voices emanating from a box in the family home. Leave the population rudderless, if only temporarily, and half the battle is won. Much the same applies to the newspapers; editorial deadlines being what they are, it is possible to mount a coup after one edition has been printed, then secure the newspaper offices (if that is the aim) before the next edition is made up.

The reader will no doubt have identified a major problem at this stage; regional broadcasting stations and provincial newspapers. In a country the size of, say, the United States it would require the manpower of almost the entire army to close down every broadcasting station and this would still not prevent the use of Citizen's Band (CB) radio to spread the news, together with seditious messages that might damage the plotter's position. Even in Great

Britain there are four major provincial broadcasting areas and many other smaller ones. In a country like Great Britain, however, the majority of networks are controlled from around the capital – certainly the news programmes and Independent Radio and Television News are – so it might be possible to throw a partial blanket over the media and rely on the resulting provincial confusion to cloak one's actions. Another possibility is to cut land lines and microwave links between broadcasting units, and to destroy or temporarily disable transmitters. It wouldn't take too many men to do this, as long as they were correctly briefed and escorted by an engineer who knew what he was doing.

A more drastic measure still is that which was forced upon the Chilean military during their own coup; use the air force to bomb the transmitters and relay stations in daylight. This is a last resort as it will almost certainly lead to loss of innocent life and is very bad public relations. Such measures are to be avoided wherever possible.

Another problem worth looking at is the distribution of 'secondary target' personalities within the capital and major provincial centres. There will almost certainly be too many for the plotters to neutralize quickly, so the answer is to do a bit of detective work, preferably with the assistance of a telephone engineer; ascertain their addresses and telephone numbers and those of their offices and systematically cut the telephones off. By hampering their communications one can delay, if not prevent, the onset of 'networking' among the opposition and deny them any opportunity to present a united front.

The one problem that has not been confronted properly is that of raising a military force capable of carrying out one's own wishes. It has been implicit throughout the book so far, apart from one section, that the coup would be carried out by soldiers, sailors and airmen working under the orders of officers sympathetic to one's cause. How does one set about raising such a force? The short answer is: the force will raise itself, once the 'rightness' of the cause becomes evident to potential partners. Besides, one doesn't need the entire army on one's side to mount a successful coup.

4
MEANS
Manpower and Firepower

The manpower problem was described, in its essentials, at the end of the last Chapter. The firepower problem will be solved automatically once the manpower has been raised. The key to both problems, however, is first to select the firepower necessary to do the job and then to choose the men who have that firepower available.

Coups d'état down the years have shown how loath people are to confront tanks and armed men with their bare hands. One way to maintain calm in a tense city is to confront people not only with tanks and soldiers, but with the visible proof of your willingness to use them. Not only will the population be cowed into submission but loyalist troops may think twice before engaging you. It is vital to enforce a temporary curfew, as well. This keeps people off the streets and allows the plot to proceed with minimal interruption and no traffic jams to slow things down. If the worst comes to the worst a curfew will also ensure that a violent confrontation between plotters and loyalists does not result in civilian deaths.

So what are the requirements, in firepower terms, of a successful coup? These will vary from situation to situation, but in the very simplest terms they are: the wherewithal to eliminate bodyguards who may try to protect your human targets; the heavy weapons or equipment necessary to storm a defended strongpoint such as the presidential palace; the heavy weapons, armour and engineer stores necessary to seal off and, if necessary, defend sections of the capital

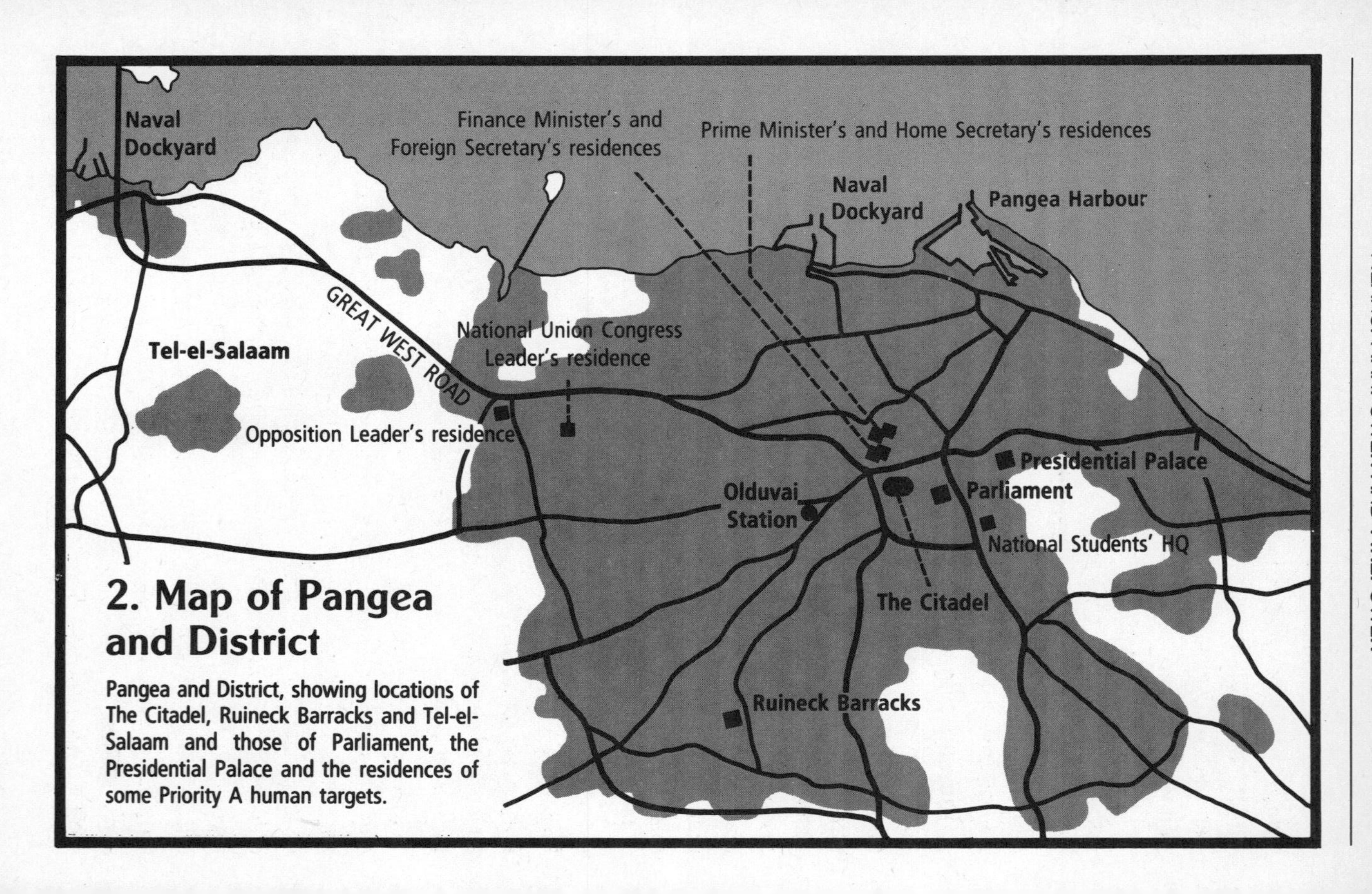

2. Map of Pangea and District

Pangea and District, showing locations of The Citadel, Ruineck Barracks and Tel-el-Salaam and those of Parliament, the Presidential Palace and the residences of some Priority A human targets.

or provincial centre concerned against loyalist counter-attack; the vehicles and manpower necessary to maintain a high-profile deterrent presence on the streets; the manpower and vehicles necessary to get quickly to broadcasting organizations or specific and dispersed point targets and secure these.

It is obvious from this short summary that a coup might be as complex a military operation as a brigade-size attack in a conventional war, and officers with the initials PSC (for *Passed Staff College*) after their names will be better able to cope with the complexity of this particular command and control exercise.

The adjoining map of a major city shows just how complex the operation could be. Marked on the map are the major institutions targeted for neutralization as well as the homes and offices of politicians, union leaders and other personalities, and their dispersal demonstrates the difficulty of keeping control over the first echelon of troops going about their primary and secondary tasks. For the sake of convenience we should assume that all the apparatus of modern political power, including broadcasting stations, is concentrated in this one (fictitious) city, Pangea, capital of Gondwanaland.

It would be a waste of the reader's time to go through an exhaustive list of the exact hardware necessary at this stage; better by far to begin by describing the man who ought to be doing the detailed military planning. This man, whoever he may be, holds the key to the success of the entire enterprise because in a coup, planning counts for everything.

Ideally the planner will be a senior officer of the rank of colonel or above. He will have passed staff college; he will have commanded successfully a battalion, at the very least, and preferably on active service. He will be known to and respected by junior officers and enlisted men and will have their trust. He will be able to foresee the logistic, command and control and operational problems likely to be encountered and should be able to state clearly the plotters' requirements in terms of Intelligence, firepower and equipment. If such a man does not already belong to the immediate cadre of plotters, he must be invited to join, given that he is sympathetic to the coup's aims and is willing to take part. Here the real manpower problem becomes manifest: subverting pesonnel without either telling them too much or making oneself vulnerable to the government's security services.

CHOOSING A LEADER

Let us assume that it is necessary to subvert the planner (the plotters may, after all, be a clique of politicians or businessmen with no military knowledge, or junior/middle-ranking officers with insufficient weight to carry out the coup). The problems involved in subverting this officer are a microcosm of the problems faced in subverting other personnel who may be able to bring whole units to your assistance or neutralize them during the coup itself.

It must first be established whether or not he would be in favour of a coup d'état. This is easier to do then some might think. It is quite possible that some of the plotters are close to him, either socially or else serving under him. Officers do talk to one another; the person chosen to sound him out may be familiar with his feelings towards the present government. If not, it should be easy enough to form a rough estimate of his views without incriminating oneself.

Problems can arise, however, if there are two or three likely candidates for the job, especially if, despite their military and personal qualifications, there is no firm knowledge of their feelings and likely response to an approach. No matter how many candidates there may be, however, a number of points must be determined before any approach is made – a number of questions must be answered satisfactorily.

• **Are their political views sympathetic to your own?** In other words, are they politically motivated enough to harbour strong feelings about the present government's policies and actions, and, more importantly, do they disagree with the government? The answer to this question must be Yes.

• **Do they see any likelihood of change for the better in the immediate future?** Put another way, do they have any faith in the democratic process's ability to throw up another government which will do better? Or, if the regime is already a military one, is there any likelihood that other members of the junta or supreme military council will bring pressure to bear in order to improve things? The answer to this question must be No.

• **Is the candidate bound to the present government by ties of ethnic loyalty or by loyalty to a powerful patron within the upper echelons?** Does the candidate have any good reason not to want a coup (other than constitutional ones)? Will his position be made more vulnerable, for example, if a different tribal bloc is in the ascendancy? The answer to these questions must be No.

• **Would the candidate welcome the advancement of his own particular tribal or ethnic bloc?** To put it crudely, if the candidate is, for example, a Muslim in the predominantly Christian army of a country polarized within itself between Christian and Muslim – and which he perceives to be misruled by the Christians – does he feel strongly enough about the issue to abandon principles of national unity and make a bid for Muslim supremacy? The answer must be Yes – though this may be difficult to establish if he is inclined to be circumspect.

• **Is he satisfied with his career pattern so far?** Doctor Luttwak has established, quite rightly, that the motivation for many officers involved in a coup d'état is dissatisfaction with the armed forces – more accurately, a perceived inability on their part to acknowledge their (the officers') worth and reward it adequately. So, is our candidate bitter at having been passed over repeatedly for promotion? Or is he an impatient high-flyer who wants to climb the ladder of success quickly? The answer to this question must be Yes. Bear in mind, however, that a much passed-over officer may, in fact, be incompetent and therefore a liability to the plotters.

• **Is the candidate's sense of duty towards his country offended by the politicians running it (whether they are in uniform or not)?** Does the candidate feel that, sooner or later, somebody must do something about the mess we're in? The answer must be Yes.

The short checklist above is imperfect because it fails to take into account factors peculiar to the armed forces of a given country in a particular set of circumstances. It will certainly be necessary to re-word some of these questions, or ask others, in the light of specific circumstances, but the principles outlined above (and explored in more depth by both Luttwak and Finer) still hold good. Only when the likely candidates have been observed closely and the questions answered satisfactorily is it possible to make a choice between them and, eventually, approach one of them. Whether or not the other candidates are approached also will depend very much on the degree of expertise required, and the particular benefits the other candidates can bring to the coup in terms of units under command, detailed knowledge of the area of operations or intimacy with the head of state's timetable.

It is important to stress here that we have been talking about an operational commander only, not a political leader. It is probable that the political leader is already at the centre of the plot, in which case all he requires is a lieutenant (what the Americans would call an 'Executive Officer') who will do more or less what he is told. The problem with a man in this officer's position is that he needs to know a great deal if he is to carry out his planning and command the task properly. The more he knows the greater a danger he is to the plotters. Knowledge is power and he will have to be given enough knowledge to make him a potential usurper of the plotters' position. This is a risk which must be taken. The only way to minimize it is by selecting somebody without too much political ambition, or else to offer him a share of the power the coup will bring, and then ensure that he is in no position afterwards to increase his own share of that commodity.

Whoever the planner is, one of his immediate tasks must be to work out exactly what is required to overthrow the government as quickly and finally as possible, and to consolidate the new regime's status with the minimum of resistance, organized or otherwise. A rough list of the manpower and equipment necessary to secure the city mentioned above is given elsewhere in this Chapter. Similar lists must be drawn up for other key points within the country and a priority established for each target. There will be three priorities: A, B and C, each corresponding roughly to the various phases of the coup itself.

Priority A targets will be 'taken out' during the Assault Phase of the operation; Priority B targets during the Continuation Phase of the coup; Priority C targets can wait until the Consolidation Phase. It is worth mentioning at this point something which will be covered in more detail later on; the various phases will not necessarily run into each other in a smooth sequence across the country. The Assault Phase may last only five minutes where abduction of the head of state is concerned, but perhaps two hours if an airport or dock must be secured. Elements of the team charged with 'taking out' the head of state may have passed on to the Continuation Phase of their series of tasks before the Airport Control teams have finished their Assault Phase. But this lies very much in the future on our plotters' time-scale.

THE SELECTION PROCESS

Of more immediate interest is the problem of deciding who is available to assist the coup and who will be implacably hostile. Among the latter will probably be the national secret service or Intelligence agencies and the police force. Others who may be reckoned to be foe rather than friend are likely to include presidential or royal guard units (almost invariably selected for their personal or institutional loyalty to the person they are there to protect) and, quite possibly, anti-terrorist units of either the police, paramilitary forces or army.

In a country with deep ethnic divisions, troops from the same tribal or religious bloc as the head of state are liable to feel greater loyalty to him than to the plotters. This must be borne in mind, especially in racially integrated armies. In a country like India, whose army is not particularly well integrated; or South Africa, where there are quite clear distinctions between white, black and coloured units and between Permanent Force and Citizen Force units and between these and the home defence Commando units, the element of choice is denied to the plotters. This is not necessarily a bad thing. Potential opposition is clearly identified, and obvious differences between loyalist and rebel soldiers (skin colour, presence or absence of tribal or caste marks and so on) will differentiate between friend and foe.

A racially integrated army of the kind found in Europe and parts of Africa presents a particular problem. It becomes important to select particular figures in each unit whom one may try to subvert using the checklist set out earlier, then rely on them to bring the rest of the unit over to the coup or else prevent it becoming an effective opposition. This, for obvious reasons, is a more dangerous situation and the only balm is the solidarity felt by soldiers for one another. In a fully integrated army there is no obvious motive for one unit to open fire on another, as there might be in a segregated army, so the likelihood of intervention by those units not suborned will tend to be lower. For a start, there will be considerable confusion as to what exactly is happening. Secondly, if a feeling of dissatisfaction with the government is prevalent throughout the armed forces, anybody guessing what has happened may not feel inclined to jeopardize his own career under the new government by sticking his neck out. Finally, armies are trained to fight other armies, not their own. Uncommitted units will probably adopt a cautious 'wait-and-see' attitude before declaring themselves one way or the other. Of course, in doing nothing, they are making a *de facto* declaration of passive support for the plotters.

Bearing these problems in mind, then, where does one start? The letters PSC after the officer's name start to mean something at this point. Timing is crucial and so are logistics, so it is logical to use, if possible, units stationed near their intended targets. If they have been infiltrated by the secret service there will be less time for the government to react to the 'Go' order when it is given, and proximity to the target(s) means that the troops will preserve the vital element of surprise. As an aside it is worth noting that the Chilean coup of September 1973 did not enjoy total surprise because units moving up to Santiago by truck were spotted at midnight on the 10th, eight hours before H-Hour. It would have been far more logical to use units stationed around Santiago. One can probably ascribe this error to the plotters' desire to present Allende with a united front and, in effect, a *fait accompli.*

Returning briefly to the map on page 62, how do we set about maintaining surprise, short lines of communication and logistic simplicity? There are three major troop concentrations around and within Pangea: at the Citadel, symbolic centre of the nation and the base of the Tectonic Knights, Gondwanaland's equivalent of the British Household Cavalry; at Ruineck Barracks, on the outskirts of the city but only twenty minutes' drive from the centre; and at Tel-el-Salaam, the largest garrison town and headquarters of the army, thirty kilometres due west of the city. For the purpose of this exercise let us assume that there is no national guard or gendarmerie in Gondwanaland, but that the civil police are armed.

How reliable are the Tectonic Knights? Are they likely to join the plot? If not are any of their officers or key personnel sympathetic to its aims? Ideally, the Knights would be the spearhead of the coup, charged with taking out the majority of Priority A targets because they could reach any part of Pangea within minutes and with total surprise. If the Knights cannot be counted on to join, they must be neutralized. The next best option is Ruineck Barracks. Troops there, being ordinary line infantry, armour, artillery and support troops, may have less loyalty to the head of state. Given the right sort of assistance from covert teams operating within the capital, they could secure Priority A and B targets quickly and easily. And Tel-el-Salaam? Given a reasonable number of friendly units there, the army headquarters itself could be sealed off while a contingent races towards the capital to take the airport and certain Priority B and rather more Priority C targets. Other units could be dispatched from there to the out-of-town residences of Priority A human targets during the Assault Phase.

The prospect of doing things the other way round, with units rushing into town from Tel-el-Salaam, possibly to confront the Tectonic Knights and the Ruineck garrison if the plot has been compromised, is far less attractive. Quite apart from the certain loss of surprise involved, it is highly likely that an unacceptably large proportion of the force will have to secure the Citadel and Ruineck Barracks to keep the troops there under control. Even if they have been technically neutralized, there is always the possibility of trouble breaking out. It has been assumed that the majority of uncommitted troops will remain so, of course, but maintaining security in a rapidly expanding group of plotters has never been easy; besides, if somebody manages to get to a telephone to warn the Knights and the Commandant at Ruineck, even the swiftest, best-executed Assault Phase may be vulnerable to a sharp response. It is much safer to try, if possible, to subvert military units closest to the geographical centre of the coup. Loyalist troops driving or flying in from anywhere farther away than Tel-el-Salaam will arrive too late to prevent the coup; they can be ignored for the time being.

WAYS AND MEANS

In terms of firepower and equipment we shall probably need the following to take out our Priority A targets.

• **Human targets** Small arms (rifles, submachine-guns and pistols) with which to kill the bodyguards and threaten the targets themselves; vehicles in which to travel to the target's residence or place of work and to convey him to a secure area; VHF or HF (preferably the former) radio sets with which to communicate with the plotters' HQ; enough men equipped with small arms, light or medium machine-guns (LMG, MMG) and light anti-armour weapons (LAW) to guard the place, if it is a ministry or place of work, in order to prevent loyalists taking it over again and claiming a degree of moral ascendancy from its possession.

• **Buildings** Small arms again, for the reasons stated above and also to cow the occupants into submission; light and medium machine-guns and LAW to defend the building from within, if necessary; enough men to garrison the building and to guard those occupants who have not been removed for safe-keeping; vehicles to get the men there, remove the key personnel and carry defence stores and ammunition; defence (or engineer) stores with which to cordon off the area, mount roadblocks and erect anti-tank and anti-personnel barriers; such heavy weapons (primarily anti-tank weapons, whether mounted on armoured fighting vehicles ((AFV)) or not) as are necessary to defend the locality. The use of mortars up to 81mm calibre may be considered, but is not to be encouraged; mortars are not particularly accurate and their proper control during a street battle (what the British Army calls FIBUA – Fighting in Built-Up Areas) is problematic. Use of mortars may not endear the plotters to the population who must suffer their effects. The same applies to artillery.

• **Major facilities** To take over a radio station or airfield is not the simplest business in the world. Bursting into a studio while the disc jockey is on the air so that the population can hear him being forcibly removed or, worse, shot (as happened in Chile) not only gives warning that something is up, it is bad public relations. Similarly, one doesn't shoot up the control tower of an airport – the air traffic controller may succeed in getting a message to those aircraft within radio range. One requires equipment basically similar to that used for taking out a building, but one must have a team of signals experts on hand to close the station down or to run it for the plotters. It may be stating the obvious, but there is a good case for carrying out the coup while these facilities are off the air in any case. Telephone exchanges never close down, of course, but they can be controlled easily enough by a small team assisted by a signals group and a sympathetic telephone engineer. In the case of the airport one further requirement is for vehicles to be scattered about on the runways and the grass verges to prevent the landing of tactical transport aircraft such as the Lockheed C-130 Hercules or Shorts Skyvan, which might be used to land loyalist troops or foreigners coming to the aid of the government. If elements of the air force have joined the coup it is possible that they will assume responsibility for air traffic control and air defence, especially if they have combat aircraft available.

• **Ports and Frontiers** Elements of the navy may assist in securing the nation's ports. If not, both they and naval dockyards must be secured. The equipment necessary for doing so will match that described above, but it is worth adding artillery or heavy mortars and threatening with bombardment any ship's master who wishes to weigh anchor. Frontiers need guarding both to prevent fugitives escaping and to prevent the government's allies invading. Security at normal border crossings must be stepped up, naturally, but equally important is the patrolling by land and air of the frontiers in order to deter possible escape attempts and to give early warning of possible invasion. Long coastlines need both air and surface patrols; the former can be carried out by air force or army aviation units, if necessary, but the latter demands the navy's expertise. Land and sea frontiers, however, fit more comfortably into Priority C so there is little point in worrying about them at this stage.

Priority B and C targets are likely to be much like Priority A targets: people, buildings and facilities. The difference is that they are less crucial to the coup as a whole and, in any case, by the time they are tackled much of the potential for organized resistance will have evaporated so fewer resources in manpower and firepower need be devoted to them. Indeed, depending on the nature of the targets, one may be quite justified in splitting up task groups after the Assault Phase and assigning each sub-group to a secondary target (Priority B at the highest), leaving a cadre at the Priority A target to defend it. In all probability there simply won't be enough troops to make any other course of action possible.

Remember that we have discussed only the requirements, so far, not what is available. Much of what we need will be available at any barracks or garrison: men, small arms, trucks and light vehicles, radios. Engineer stores and armour are the biggest problem. The engineers at Ruineck Barracks are bound to have the heavy plant and equipment necessary to erect temporary but effective barriers. The signals group there or at the Citadel will furnish much of our communications equipment, but manpack radios will be more plentiful at the infantry and signals stores in Ruineck; so also will LMGs, MMGs and LAWs. The artillery group at Ruineck will provide manpower, vehicles and radios (as well as a highly tuned system of organization), but may need to be devoted to the docks and airfield, providing a deterrent to anyone wishing to sail or fly in or out of the area. The military police (MP) group at both Ruineck and the Citadel can assist with traffic control or the movement and guarding of prisoners, while ordnance will supply vehicles and manpower; the medics will stand by for possible emergencies, taking over whatever hospitals are deemed suitable.

If the Tectonic Knights are on our side what can they provide? Small arms and manpower, to be sure, but also light armoured vehicles; even the Tectonic Knights (like the British Household Cavalry) have a war role in addition to their special role at the Citadel and may even have their own stocks of live ammunition for the AFVs. Of course these are more likely to be scout or reconnaissance vehicles than tanks, but the psychological effect on both the population and the various human targets of having large, armed monsters roaming the streets will be salutary. It would be a mistake not to use them. The Knights should be allocated a number of Priority A targets which dismounted troops can secure while the AFVs take up positions nearby to dominate the area.

What about heavy armour? A regiment of tanks is based at Ruineck; how should they be used? Once deployed on city streets, tanks should be used in this context for static defence, taking over from the Knights' AFVs and allowing them and the regiment's own recce squadron to begin patrolling or move on to other targets.

AFV and artillery ammunition might present something of a problem. It is probable, but not certain, that first-line scales of ammunition are kept at each HQ. More ammunition than this should not be required, but if it is where does it come from? If sufficient ammunition for the Assault Phase is unavailable, how does one get hold of it? The majority of stocks are probably in an ordnance depot; if not at Tel-el-Salaam, then at some other remote spot. If this is the case (and it certainly is in the British Army – weapons and ammunition are kept well apart), there is much to be said for leaving the armour and artillery out of the Assault Phase entirely or, if the depot is within easy reach, using gunners and tank crews in the infantry role to take out the depot as a Priority A target. If they can do this successfully they not only get their hands on the necessary ammunition, but they deny it to loyalist units.

If the ordnance depot is at Tel-el-Salaam it will be necessary either to control it or neutralize it, denying the ammunition to anyone. Alternatively, one could subvert armour and artillery units there and use them in the city during the Continuation and Consolidation Phases, relying on infantry with small arms to carry out the Assault Phase.

The previous few pages give some idea of the complexity of a coup and the need for careful planning. The various factors and unknown quantities described above must be weighed and balanced by the planners in the light of the availability or otherwise of different units and their capabilities. The planning process, which has begun with an appreciation of what exactly is necessary to secure the capital and seize the reins of government moves on to the problem of raising the forces necessary to do it. The fictional Pangea must serve again.

One will by now have some idea of which units not to approach. The Tectonic Knights may be fiercely loyal to the government. If so, ignore them; it would be a huge mistake to approach one of their officers. This problem is endemic in most countries. In Nigeria, for example, it may be easier to get Northern officers to join a plot against a Southern head of state than one of their own (though not necessarily; the January 1986 plot against President Ibrahim Babangida, himself a middle-belt Northerner, was initiated by what one observer describes as 'The Northern Mafia', a militant clique of mainly Hausa officers. The plot was discovered before a coup could take place); in South Africa it may be easier to suborn the voluntary-service Commandos, who are liable to be less liberal than the Permanent or Citizen Force units, if one wants to overthrow a comparatively liberal regime and install something closer to the purist's view of apartheid. In the Middle East it may be easier to suborn Shiite Muslim troops than Sunni or Wahhabi; so it is in Pangea. Let us assume that the Tectonic Knights are recruited from a particular region and its officers from a particular class. One's only chance of inhibiting their ability to counter the plot is to subvert a disaffected trooper or infantryman – or better still a technician – who can lose the garage or armoury keys at the right moment.

THE PROCESS OF SUBVERSION

For the main part let us concentrate on the other units nearby. Let us assume that they have not disqualified themselves through regional, ethnic, religious or personal loyalty – how do we subvert them? The answer is to start by sounding out one medium-ranking officer, perhaps a senior company commander, whom one of the plotters knows fairly well. He must be investigated using the checklist set out above and, when he has satisfied as many requirements as are deemed necessary, he can be approached directly. This is the most delicate moment in any subversion and must be handled carefully. It is probably enough just to intimate that there may be something in the offing and that the officer should hold himself ready, but keep his mouth shut. Alternatively, he could be told bluntly that he will be required to take a particular part in a forthcoming coup but that orders will not be given for some time. The problem here is to suck him in so that he not only wants the coup to take place but has a vested interest in not revealing the whole thing to his commanding officer or to the Intelligence services.

Should he be told which other officers are involved or is it better to use the cell system and leave him with only one point of contact? Depending on the man, one could do either. A young officer who is not too sure of himself and who needs the family solidarity of a regimental officers' mess may feel crushed by the burden of loneliness created by his secret. He would be a liability, but it may be an acceptable risk to name one or two other conspirators within his own unit simply to show him that he is not alone. This is only worth doing, however, if the officer is a key figure within the unit being subverted or neutralized. But, on the whole, such men should not be approached. A more self-sufficient officer – a company commander or adjutant – will have fewer self-doubts, while a battalion or regimental commander should have the personal stature to carry the secret and, come the glorious day, bring his unit along with him. Ideally, one would approach the commanding officer first, thus cutting out a great deal of hard work and reducing the risks, but there is an added risk in approaching a senior officer: loyalty, tradition and a sense of duty – remember that he will have been selected for promotion by the very Establishment one is trying to overthrow. He may feel some responsibility towards them, whatever his personal or political views.

Selecting one's initial contact within a particular unit is very important. The right man must be self-sufficient enough to carry his secret, and trustworthy enough (from the plotters' point of view) to give reliable advice as to who else in the unit may be approached safely and whether or not to approach the commanding officer. He should not approach the others himself, though, because the key to security is compartmentalization within the group of plotters. This may make liaison between various units cumbersome, but it is the price one must pay for success.

Exactly which officers within a unit does one approach? Much depends on the complexion of the plotters and the militancy of the officer corps as a whole, but one should aim, if possible, for the top: the company commanders, adjutant, motor transport officer, signals officer and quartermaster. If one can subvert the commanding officer as well, so much the better. If not, his place must be taken on the day by the senior company commander, unless the CO himself is willing to take part when confronted with the subversion of his entire unit. This is probably unlikely because no senior officer would enjoy having his *amour propre* dealt so public a blow. These officers and their subordinate platoon commanders will be able to bring almost the entire battalion or regiment over to the plot. If the unit is divided between separate (and possibly quite distant) company or platoon locations, one can subvert the local commanders as well, knowing that there will be less peer pressure on them from the rest of the unit if the unit as a whole has not been subverted. Besides, offering a young, keen officer his own independent command is good psychology, especially when he knows that there is little chance of interference from 'the Boss'.

Once the senior echelons in a given unit have been subverted as far as is safely possible, 'safe' officers of a more junior rank can be let into the plot after their loyalties have been investigated. Even senior NCOs could be admitted; NCOs command more respect than officers on occasion, and in an army where the status of the NCO is high, it is possible that doubtful soldiers will turn to their platoon sergeant or company sergeant-major for confirmation of totally unexpected orders from a young and inexperienced officer.

So much for the units joining the plot. What about the units that won't? The term 'neutralization' has been used – what does it mean? What it means is not annihilation but the imposition of a temporary impotence. It was suggested, not entirely tongue in cheek, that a disaffected trooper or infantryman might be induced to 'lose' the garage or armoury keys and so keep the Tectonic Knights out of the way temporarily. In today's high-technology armed forces it would not require much more than this to paralyze a unit. Consider; most sub-units of company level or thereabouts have their own weapons store and a garage for their vehicles. With AFVs and small arms locked away and ammunition kept in a separate magazine, the units are impotent if they cannot get access to these weapons. If, in addition, telephone and radio contact with the outside world is severed, not only will the unit not receive a timely warning that something is afoot, but will probably take so long to react that they will be able to do little to prevent or change the course of events.

In the case of the Tectonic Knights, for example, one has only to disconnect civil and military network telephones and any radios within easy reach at the appropriate moment, seal off all exits from the Citadel and try, if possible, to ensure that the keys to the garage, armouries and ammunition magazines really are lost. Pouring a modern 'super-glue' into a lock will often substitute adequately for 'losing' the keys, if it proves impossible to gain access to them. This may set off intruder alarms, but it will be too late. If access to the alarm control system is available, so much the better, but this cannot be relied on.

This raises the planners' Intelligence problem, if only briefly at this stage. Given that a unit will not join the coup, how is it to be neutralized? The people in a position to know are liable to be a handful of senior NCOs and senior officers. The Intelligence Requirement is to discover their identity if the plotters haven't this information already. When the person or persons who have the required information are identified the information must be wormed out of them or they must be induced to join the plot. The neutralization problem may indeed be solved just by misappropriating the armoury keys, but the solution may equally involve something more complicated such as a covert raid aimed at securing the Citadel's guardroom and then placing the entire Corps of Knights under guard.

The rest of the Intelligence problem will be dealt with in the next Chapter. Let it just be said here that it is bigger than many would suspect. It encompasses every area of the operation, from the likely response of other units in the army, navy and air force to the movements of key human targets, from getting their telephone numbers (if ex-directory) to learning what time broadcasting staff leave the local TV and radio stations at the end of the working day. The Intelligence requirement will not be defined properly until the planning is under way and particular information is required. At this point the Intelligence Cycle begins and behaves as a self-sustaining system until after the coup itself: Intelligence Requirement; Information Gathering; Collation; Dissemination; then Intelligence Requirement again.

WORST AND BEST CASES

The reader will no doubt wonder why it is necessary to mobilize whole regiments of tanks and artillery and up to a brigade of troops simply to 'take out' a handful of unarmed civilians. The purpose of going into such depth is to illustrate the 'worst case' scenario – the overthrow of a firmly entrenched government in the face of considerable potential opposition from loyalist units of the army. Argentina provided an excellent illustration of the 'worst case', an attempted coup which took place in June 1955. The coup, initiated by the Argentine Navy, began with an aerial bombardment of the Presidential Palace, the Casa Rosada, in which President Juan Peron was (he thought) firmly established. Simultaneously the façade of the building was raked by heavy machine-gun fire from the Navy Ministry nearby, while a contingent of marines began to assault the Casa Rosada on foot. Peron called up army troops with tanks and artillery who repelled the marines, then went on to shell the ministry, whose occupants surrendered soon after. The bombing and strafing continued until the naval air base was overrun by the army.

The coup failed for a number of reasons: one was the ten minutes' warning Peron had received of the air attack which allowed him to take cover and to call for loyal army reinforcements (thus illustrating the importance of security and the critical nature of a coup's timings); a second reason was bad weather – fog, which had grounded some of the aircraft and, more importantly, had delayed an amphibious landing near Buenos Aires by marine reinforcements. A third reason was the duplicity of the Argentine Air Force whose leaders had intimated to the navy plotters that they would join in – they didn't.

An earlier coup in 1944, also in Argentina, illustrates the 'best case'. The then-President, Ramirez, decided that Argentina should no longer be aligned with the Japan-Germany-Italy axis; the Argentine Generals were infuriated by this decision and, led by Peron and Vice-President Brigadier-General Edelmiro Farrell, a contingent of them walked into the President's office in the Casa Rosada and forced him at pistol-point to resign in favour of Farrell. This example illustrates how easy it can be to take power in a country where power is centralized and concentrated largely in the hands of one man. The difference between the two coups is enormous. In the one, a couple of pistols in the hands of men visibly determined to use them if necessary was the only firepower required; in the other it was necessary either to have the army and air force as an ally (the latter took very little part in the coup attempt, on either side) or to out-gun them. The 1955 coup illustrates also the importance of a joint services approach to a coup d'état if possible. While a soldier may not open fire on his comrade or on a civilian, inter-service rivalry being what it is (and the visual distinction between different services' uniforms being what that is), a soldier may have few doubts about opening fire on a sailor or airman if the order to do so seems a reasonable one.

We have looked at the Manpower/Firepower problem in sufficient depth so far. We have identified the means by which individuals and entire units may be subverted and the need to select them carefully, for their particular capabilities in the context of a coup d'état. We have identified the requirement to neutralize loyalist or uncommitted units and the need for adequate and timely Intelligence about these and other targets. What we have not done is to discuss two particular factors in our planning: seniority within the armed forces of the plotters, and the absence of any national troops in the plot.

The Chilean coup of 1973 and other coups which have taken place elsewhere, have been characterized by almost complete unanimity between the different branches of the armed forces, and by the stature of the men leading the coups. In Chile, for example, the figurehead of the coup was none other than the Commander-in-Chief of the army, General Pinochet; his confederates were the Commanders-in-Chief of the Chilean Navy and Air Force. There was no need to subvert officers (most were heartily sick of the government); Pinochet and his colleagues had merely to give orders. This pattern is common to coup attempts where the senior echelons of the military are unanimous in their view of the government and the need to replace it quickly. In such a situation the full resources of the armed forces are available from the very start and the lead time between a plot being conceived and its eventual execution can be very short – less than a week in the case of the Chilean coup.

The question of using mercenaries simply doesn't arise, unless the armed forces of the country concerned are so puny, and the targets to be tackled so few and so lightly defended, that a small mercenary force can be raised discreetly. A large mercenary force is so conspicuous, unless some friendly government is supporting and hiding it, that its existence and then its mission ceases to be a secret. Nevertheless, the number of small, independent states with limited military and economic resources and no super-power sponsorship is quite large, and these states are vulnerable to a well-planned and properly executed coup d'état by a small, professional mercenary force. The planning of such a coup will not differ in any significant detail (save that of scale) from the outline given above, except in two particular areas – recruitment of mercenaries (which is not part of this book) and the logistical problem of getting them into the target area.

The best friend a mercenary force can have is a friendly government close to the target. This government will provide a secure jumping-off point and may even assist with training, weapons, equipment and personnel, if only by turning a blind eye to what is happening in its own backyard.

Perhaps the strongest lesson to be drawn from this Chapter is the importance of Intelligence. Accurate, timely Intelligence makes the planning problem much easier. It allows the plotters to tailor their plan to the operational requirements, and their manpower and logistics to the plan. We shall explore the Intelligence requirement in more detail in the next Chapter.

5
MEANS
Planning

The planning stage of a coup d'état is the most critical. The previous Chapter discussed the problems of finding a planner, then finding the manpower and firepower needed to carry out the coup. In a sense this was a little like putting the cart before the horse because until some detailed planning has been done it is impossible to state one's requirements with any real accuracy. Nevertheless, it was important also to describe some of the constraints within which the planners must work; if politics is the art of the possible, then so is the coup d'état. Only when one's friends have been identified (and, perhaps more importantly, one's enemies) is it possible to proceed with some clear idea of what it is possible to achieve.

The first stage in the planning process is to select the Priority A and B targets for the Assault Phase of the coup. To do this requires as much in the way of political as of military experience, and it is here that political and military planners must liaise most closely. A thorough knowledge of the machinery of government is essential, as is a well-developed political instinct. As stated earlier, it is vital to know who must be neutralized before it is possible to say truthfully that the country can be placed under the plotters' full control.

Much will depend on the extent to which members of the Establishment are involved in the coup. If the entire cabinet is involved, it may be necessary only to seize the president, prime minister, or monarch. If the coup is aimed at overthrowing the entire

Establishment, the pool of potential targets is far bigger and some care must be used in their selection and classification. Let us begin by looking at some of the key figures in two very different types of government, presidential and prime ministerial.

In a *presidential* type of government, the head of state (who may be a monarch or a president) has executive powers; so have members of his cabinet; so have junior ministers or secretaries of state. Senior civil servants have wide-reaching powers which may or may not be used in support of the ministers they serve.

In a *prime ministerial* type of government, the head of state may have only symbolic powers or a ceremonial role. A change of government under this system means replacement of the prime minister, the cabinet and junior ministers. Senior civil servants in either system should serve successive ministers with the same degree of impartiality. However politically astute they may be, civil servants tend to keep out of the sordid business of politics if they possibly can. Thus the constant factors in this system are the head of state and the civil service.

In a presidential government, then, the decision-making process begins right at the top. The head of state must be removed, along with those ministers in a position to offer concrete resistance to the coup: the minister for defence; the interior minister (or home secretary), who normally controls the police and paramilitary forces as well as the national security or counter-Intelligence service; the foreign minister, who normally controls the secret service; the deputies of these people; and the president or monarch's own personal staff, including the head of state's spouse and any children in a position to rally resistance or be used by loyalists as a symbol of resistance to the coup.

The targets in a prime ministerial government will be much the same; a question hangs over the head of state, however. Should the monarch or president be removed as well or is it best to leave him or her in place as a symbol of continuity and, in spite of appearances to the contrary, national stability? Much depends on the head of state's popularity within the country as a whole and, of course, the plotters' own views on the individual or institution concerned. As a general rule, it is best to leave a non-executive head of state alone and try to win him over to one's own point of view. In doing so you may be able to convince a greater number of the population than otherwise would have accepted the wisdom of your actions. Many coups are aimed, of course, at doing away with the monarchy altogether or at seizing the president's or monarch's title and then wielding executive powers. If this is the case, the current head of state's relationship with the institution of government must be gauged carefully. There is no sense in 'taking out' a non-executive monarch if one doesn't simultaneously take out the executive members of government who may oppose this move.

Who else, outside the immediate circle of high-profile government figures, wields enough power to be a threat to the coup? The senior commanders of the armed forces, paramilitary forces and police may not be part of your plot. Do they need neutralization? Quite possibly, yes. How strong are the trades (labour) unions? Could they mobilize public opinion against the coup? Again, yes – if their freedom is such that they have managed to build up a worthwhile power base strong enough to make them worth courting by sympathetic politicians who need their political support. So the highest-profile union leaders must be neutralized.

What about big business? It is not impossible that captains of industry will be hostile to a government resulting from a coup, though capital has a quite different constituency from labour. Should industrialists be neutralized? Absolutely not! They are too vital to the economic well-being of the country to be mishandled; they should be wooed, persuaded, kept happy. They should be treated as friends, as far as possible, and it should be made clear to them that they are being treated as friends. Once the new government is consolidated the situation may change, but for the time being leave the capitalists well alone.

Luttwak postulates a 'Strong Man' theory, in which a sizeable chunk of real power lies in the hands of a man not obviously associated with either government or labour and who appears to have no direct access to the levers of power. The leaders of minority political parties – especially those who may hold the key to political power in some sort of coalition – are typical figures, as are semi-retired 'elder statesmen' who command huge respect from both the country and their own political party. Well-developed political instincts will help identify such men; in certain cases their power will be more direct, but channelled through a system which runs parallel to, but not as part of, the constitutional government. In South Africa the upper echelons of the Afrikaner secret society, the Broederbond, would have to be neutralized if a coup seemed to represent a threat to their entrenched interests; in Israel or in certain Islamic countries militant clerics would have to be muzzled in some way (the same applies, incidentally, to Ireland!). In the southern states of America it would be necessary to neutralize the leadership of the Ku Klux Klan, and in the United Kingdom it might even be necessary to take on the Freemasons.

In short, any individual or power bloc likely to oppose the new government or resist the coup itself must be a potential target (see pages 48–50).

Having identified the human targets, what about institutions and facilities? Possession, they say, is nine points of the law; simply occupying a public building of symbolic importance, such as the presidential palace, the ministry of defence, the interior ministry, the treasury building and the national assembly or congress building, can lend a surprising air of respectability to a coup d'état, lending legitimacy, even a kind of moral ascendency, to the enterprise. The buildings to be taken over must, however, be those with symbolic as well as strategic value, the façades and structures which appear on the national TV news or which feature in tourist brochures. In America one would naturally seize the Pentagon, the Capitol and the White House; in England one would seize Buckingham Palace, 10, Downing Street, the Palace of Westminster and every major building in Whitehall, including the Horse Guards, London District's Army headquarters.

Symbolism apart, what value do these buildings hold for the plotters? They all contain their own communications facilities and, in most cases, are the nerve-centres of the armed forces, police and security forces. Besides, it is within these buildings that major decisions of national importance are made, so the people, tools and information necessary for the decision-making process are concentrated in them. There will probably be secure communications facilities within them and between them; these will be vital during the Assault Phase of the coup and will make the Continuation and Consolidation Phases much easier.

BLINDING AND DEAFENING

Any media for mass communication must be seized before the loyalists get their hands on them. Newspapers can be ignored for the time being as a properly enforced curfew in the capital and those regional centres where the coup is active will keep reporters off the street. The electronic media must be gagged and then used on the plot's behalf; this means every radio and TV station in the capital and as many as possible in the provinces. If the coup can be confined solely to the capital it may be enough to cut all telephone, telex, telegraph and satellite links between the capital (which is probably at the centre of a nationwide web of communications links) and the outside world.

It must not be forgotten that Bob Denard's attempted coup in Cotonou failed because he did not seize the national radio station, so allowing President Kerekou to appeal to his people and the armed forces to resist the mercenaries. In April 1961, the attempted coup in Algeria by four French Generals failed because President De Gaulle, in Paris, was able to appeal direct to the citizens of both Metropolitan France and Algeria to remain loyal, and – more importantly – to the *Appelés* (French Army conscripts) through the transistor radios which most of this new generation of soldier-citizens now owned. It was their withdrawal from the coup attempt which led to its downfall.

Nobody now underestimates the power which control of a broadcasting station confers, but it is worthwhile emphasizing the point.

Military targets need careful consideration. Certain units will have to be neutralized once it has been established that they are not only loyal to the government but in a position to offer solid opposition to the coup. Uncommitted units will, as stated earlier, remain on the sidelines, either trying to work out what is happening or watching to see who wins. Not until a clear winner in the fight for power begins to emerge will these units show their hand. What is important here is not to waste time and effort physically holding them off, but instead to ensure that they receive no orders from a higher command echelon to intervene against the coup. This means neutralization of those formation and regional headquarters in the immediate area of the capital or other centre where the coup's activities will be concentrated so that not only uncommitted troops are left in the dark, but hostile ones as well. A little healthy confusion on the part of these troops will serve the plotters' ends well, while ensuring that only a minimum of hostile units in a position to take *direct and immediate* action need be physically neutralized.

We have our list of targets; what we need now is a list of priorities. The most critical part of the entire operation will be the Assault Phase; during this phase, which must be completed as quickly as possible and with maximum surprise, as many Priority A targets as possible must be dealt with. In broad terms the priorities will be to seize simultaneously the head of state and/or prime minister; his most important lieutenants or supporters; the most important broadcasting stations; the communications centres of the major local military headquarters; senior military and police officers who may try to interfere; those civilian communication facilities through which telephone, telex, satellite and telegraph communications within and to and from the capital must pass; those government ministries adjudged vital to the coup for both communications and symbolic importance, and any other people or facilities, adjudged, in the light of local conditions, to be important to this particular coup d'état.

These, then, are the Priority A targets and the immediate objectives of those troops to whom they have been allocated for the Assault Phase.

Priority B targets can wait until the Continuation Phase of the coup. This phase begins immediately the Priority A targets have been taken and are secure; in many cases Priority B targets will be secondary objectives allocated to troops with a fairly simple job to carry out during the Assault Phase. As stated earlier, the two phases will overlap, dependent on how long it takes particular units to secure their Priority A targets. Targets to be taken out during the Continuation Phase will include individuals who could mobilize resistance of some kind quite quickly, though not for some hours; minor broadcasting stations and communications centres; public utilities such as gas, water and electrical services (including such elements as oil refineries and energy management systems) which might be tampered with by loyalists; railway and bus stations and, of course, sea and air ports.

The Consolidation Phase involves mainly Priority C targets: items which, though important, need not be taken immediately but which cannot be ignored indefinitely. These will include minor ministries; institutions such as the national and regional headquarters of the trades union movement, semi-autonomous governmental organizations, small ports and airfields and major transport or communications centres outside the main areas of coup activity. There will also be human targets: minor politicians, student or union leaders, and so on.

What about timings? These, as has been emphasized throughout the book so far, are very important. It should be the aim of the plotters to have completed the Assault Phase within at most a few hours (2-6 hours; if it takes longer than this the coup is on its way to failure) and the Continuation Phase within 12-18 hours. The Consolidation Phase should be well under way by the end of D-Day. It is worth pointing out that the complete (or even partial, but substantial) success of each phase makes the succeeding one an order of magnitude easier. The complete failure of the Assault Phase makes the rest of the operation largely meaningless.

Brief mention was made in the preceding Chapter of small covert teams operating in the capital and elsewhere to smooth the way for the Assault Phase. Such teams can make a remarkable amount of difference to the coup's success by going in a matter of half an hour to an hour before the main force begins operations, in order to paralyze communications in both civil and military sectors. As a prelude to the Chilean coup, for example, one officer, Brigadier-General Washington Carrasco Fernandez, apparently aided only by one army engineer and three telephone engineers inside the exchange, cut the telephones of some 1,800 key loyalists in the major provincial centre of Concepción; by decoupling a closely-knit group of pro-Allende leaders in the city, he was able to roll them up subsequently, one by one, without any of them passing a warning to another.

Covert operations of this kind can make a great deal of difference, and the selection of steady officers and men to carry them out in advance of the main force is important. Due to their covert nature the teams will be too small to take on most Priority A targets, except for certain poorly protected individuals; communications equipment must be a priority target for these teams in order to prevent the wife of target A from telephoning target B to tell him that her husband has been arrested and Mr B is next on the list. Potential targets will, by their very nature, be people with a wide range of contacts and, if they are public figures, their home and business lives are probably dominated by intrusive telephone calls. A sudden drop in telephone traffic, or a total cessation of calls of all kinds, will probably arouse suspicion, so it makes a great deal of sense to sabotage the telephone exchange during the night, when most people will be asleep, or at least in their own homes, and not expecting calls every few minutes.

In fact, from every point of view, night-time is the ideal period for carrying out a coup d'état. The majority of people will be asleep, the streets will be deserted, manning levels in most major buildings will be low, bodyguards and night staff at military headquarters will be less than fully alert (and probably under strength) and many radio stations will be off the air so that they can be seized, or their transmitters sabotaged, without alerting anyone. In an ideal world a coup would be carried out without a shot being fired. One cannot count on such good fortune, but the cardinal military night-fighting rule must be observed – silence!

Let us look at some of these factors in more detail beginning where we ended the last Chapter, with one of the most important considerations of all.

INTELLIGENCE

In the previous Chapter the Intelligence Cycle has been described in its most basic form: Requirement, Collection, Collation, Dissemination. To expand slightly, this covers the Intelligence needs of the planners concerning the movements, intentions, locations and status of the targets. Collection means finding out all there is to know about the targets without arousing suspicion. Collation involves the determining of what is important to know about the targets. Dissemination means that the planners are presented with the information they need in a timely, easily assimilated form so that they can make their plans. If they need further information based on what they already know, the cycle begins all over again.

It will be obvious to the reader that certain aspects of a coup d'état's execution take on the complexity of a major anti-terrorist 'bust' in which the target area's layout, the exact number and location of terrorists and the number, state of mind and location of any hostages must be known backwards, and the anti-terrorist troops have been rehearsed exhaustively. Planners of a coup d'état know that these luxuries of planning and prepration will be denied them – they will get one chance only to do the job properly. Is it then a good thing or a bad thing to have too much Intelligence about one's targets? In principle one cannot have too much Intelligence; the more one knows the better. On the other hand a critical, unrehearsed military operation needs to be kept simple, so the Intelligence requirement for each particular phase and target is for quality rather than quantity. Only a few things need to be known by the men on the ground, but their information must be absolutely reliable. The planners need rather more information in order to allocate resources appropriately (or to determine whether the operation is even possible, given the resources available!) so the Intelligence-gathering process must begin early and must be firmly directed so that no effort or time is wasted.

The Intelligence requirement for different targets will vary. In some cases lack of Intelligence may lead only to an irritating delay. In other areas the entire operation may be compromised by overlooking one crucial detail. Bob Denard's attempted coup in Benin is a case in point. There were a number of minor Intelligence failures throughout the operation, but these were inevitable given that the planning was carried out nearly a thousand miles away from Cotonou in a region where communications are never easy. His men succeeded in securing the airport; they reached a fire base from where they could bring effective fire to bear on the state apartments within the presidential palace – but the President wasn't there. The most important element in the entire coup d'état – the elimination of President Kerekou – was a failure simply because there was nobody on the ground who could keep an eye on him and inform the mercenaries that he wasn't where he was supposed to be. Presumably Denard knew he was taking a risk by not insisting on a last-minute report on Kerekou's movements prior to the coup attempt, but he should have given this particular Intelligence requirement a greater priority than it evidently received.

Let us look at particular requirements in more detail.

• **Human targets:** Your first Intelligence Requirements for human targets are their location and movements. You have to know where they are at particular times; you cannot take it for granted that they will follow a fixed routine (indeed for security reasons many heads of state and other public figures deliberately avoid following any routine at all). You need to know what sort of protection they enjoy – how many bodyguards, where they are at particular times, how they are equipped, when the target is most vulnerable. You need to know, in other words, where and when the target can be taken out most easily. You need to know also what capacity he has for a swift, possibly decisive, reaction to the unexpected; can he, at any time of the day or night, hit a 'Panic Button' and summon immediate support?

Once these initial questions have been answered it will be possible to draw up the outline of a plan to take the target out. Priority B targets may demand no more preparation then this (in fact, in some cases, we have been too thorough, but again let us assume that we are looking at the 'worst case'); Priority A targets, on the other hand – especially the head of state, certain ministers and any 'Strong Men' – demand more care. Once it has been decided that they should be seized at, say, their office or in their homes, you have to know the layout of the building concerned, the number and locations of entrances and exists, the location of the target himself at given times of day or night, where his bodyguards or police contingent are located, how many there are at particular times of the day or night and their willingness to fight on his behalf. It may be possible for a couple of officers to walk into his office and, quite calmly, put a gun to his head. They should not contemplate doing so, however, until they are sure that he doesn't have a bell-push beside his foot which he can use unseen to summon armed assistance.

If it is decided that he can be taken while travelling by car, for example, between home and office, what route does he take? Is it necessary to follow him because he uses a different route each day? Is the car armoured? Does it have any defensive systems? Is the driver trained in high-quality defensive driving? Does the target travel in convoy with other vehicles full of guards? Does he send out decoy vehicles to fool would-be attackers? One late head of state did none of these things: General Murtala Mohammed, Head of State of Nigeria, following the 1975 coup which toppled Major-General Yakubu Gowon during the latter's absence from the country at a meeting of the Organization for African Unity, was murdered in broad daylight on a busy street by a Lieutenant-Colonel Dimka. The attack was a classic of its kind, the Head of State's car being forced to stop by another vehicle whose occupants, including Dimka, got out and shot Mohammed at point-blank range. He had paid for his lax security with his life. In this case the coup did not succeed, but it is a salutary reminder to the rich and powerful of their own vulnerability.

Once a window of vulnerability has been identified which fits in with other planning requirements, it becomes a matter simply of working out the best *modus operandi*. There might be times when the best and simplest form of attack would be a short, sharp assault by highly trained Commandos; if they are not available some other, less perfect, method must be found and this will inevitably involve finding a window of vulnerability appropriate to the skills of, say, a platoon of infantry fresh out of basic training.

• **Public Buildings:** These will certainly have some kind of guard, if only a small group of commissionaires, policemen or plain-clothes security personnel operating a controlled-entry system at the main doors. There may also be other security guards inside, covering particular floors, offices or sensitive areas. You need to know the layout of the building, the locations of offices or communications centres of particular importance, the number of entrances and exits (ordinary and emergency), the number and location of guards and security personnel, and technical details of controlled-entry systems, if there are any. You may need also to know how easy it is to get small arms into the building in case it becomes necessary to do an 'inside job'.

You will certainly need to know how many people work there, both by day and by night, and where they can be herded together so that a watchful eye can be kept on them by the minimum of troops. You need to know how, if possible, one can cut the building off entirely from the civilian telephone network, where the nodal points are of any military, government or internal telephone service, and how to seize and control them without any word getting out.

Much the same applies to police headquarters and police stations, if it is decided that they must be seized. You need to know, in addition, the location and contents of any armouries, and garages containing specialist police vehicles and how to either silence or jam police radio transmissions.

• **Electronic Media:** Radio and television broadcasting centres are, in some ways, as difficult to control as public buildings. Take the BBC as an example. In London alone the corporation has major recording and broadcasting facilities at Bush House in The Strand, at Broadcasting House in Portland Place, at Television Centre in Shepherd's Bush and at other points throughout London and the South-East of England. The Independent Television and Radio networks in London and the South-East alone account for some dozen or so other locations, all producing news or current affairs programmes and staffed by intelligent and resourceful journalists. In the provinces there are major networks in Wales, the Midlands, the South-West, the North, Central and Northern Scotland, and Northern Ireland. How does one control all these media centres simultaneously? Obviously, it is impossible.

Your first Intelligence Requirements for the electronic media, then, are to identify the major news-gathering and dissemination centres and the regional coverage each can offer. In the case of the British independent networks, for example, the centre of the entire news effort is concentrated at the Headquarters of Independent Television News (ITN) and Independent Radio News (IRN), both based in London. The former is off the air (like the BBC Television News) between about midnight and approximately 0600 hrs, although night staff are on duty to prepare news programmes for the following morning. Radio news programmes are broadcast regularly around the clock at hourly or half-hourly intervals. Both news services have national coverage, though in the case of IRN much of the dissemination is syndicated – news is relayed to regional centres to be broadcast by local radio networks intercut with regional news.

Local broadcasting centres rely very much on London for their national and international news; isolate London and much of the capacity for regional networks to warn the country about a coup is removed. The same applies to the BBC.

One other news-gathering medium must be borne in mind – the independent news agencies such as Reuters, Associated Press and the Press Association. They operate around the clock, collecting,

3. The Electronic Media

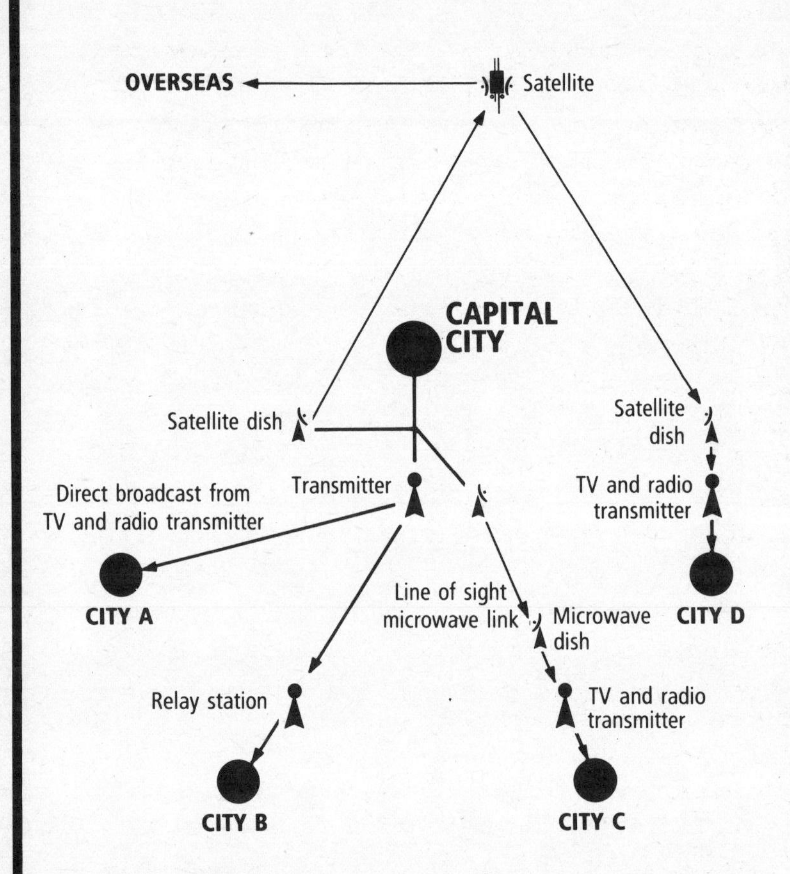

The Electronic Media (TV and radio) use a variety of broadcast and relay systems, most being radial in nature with the capital city or major broadcasting centre lying at the heart of the national network. Each system has a variety of interfaces with the main broadcasting centre and with the viewers and listeners, and each represents a potential 'choke point' which the plotter could use to his advantage, given the right quality and quantity of technical Intelligence. National newspapers and news agencies may use some of these facilities, but most will follow the models described on page 100.

processing and disseminating news and features on agency 'tapes'; their reach is both regional and international.

So your first problem is to work out how all of these agencies operate and communicate with one another and with overseas clients. Much of their news traffic is conducted by satellite, telex, telephone and radio or TV re-broadcast from relay stations around the country. You may need to know where each broadcasting centre links into a particular communications system and where this system is vulnerable from your point of view. Your intention must be to isolate the main nodal media centres from the regions; this might be done quite simply if these media use ordinary civil communications links – if not you need to know the mechanics of broadcasting and agency news dissemination.

Your next requirement is information on the broadcasting centres themselves; you need to know how to gain access and control and how to use these media to your own advantage. This means learning the layout of the centres you wish to take over (typically the major state-run TV and radio broadcasting centres), the locations of entrances and exits, the locations of transmitters and antennae if separate from the studios – along with their particular tactical features – and their power supplies, and the locations of broadcasting engineer centres where you can find specialized equipment and personnel to assist in the running of the broadcasting network. Your best ally in all this will be senior engineers in each of the major media networks who can furnish both your Intelligence Requirements and some of your skilled manpower requirements. If such a person can be subverted the coup will proceed far more smoothly; if he cannot, it may be necessary to find somebody who will assist you under duress, a time-consuming business and one that diminishes your control over the media.

Most countries have contingency plans for use of the media during a national emergency. You need to know if any exist and, if so, what they are, who is involved and what sort of hardware has been set up or earmarked for this use.

Finally, you need to know the best or most appropriate time to seize the media; it has been stated that night-time is best, and this is undoubtedly true. Television shuts down in most countries at about midnight. TV centres will be occupied by skeleton staffs and these can be dealt with easily. Many radio stations will shut down overnight, and these, again, present little trouble. Your biggest problem is all-night radio stations and news agencies. These must be isolated, though without the stations themselves going off the air, so that news of the coup doesn't reach them while they are still broadcasting. Then broadcasting centres can be taken quickly, quietly and without any panic, if desired, so that a disc jockey cannot blurt out a warning. A friendly radio engineer will be able to detail the DJ's capacity to make an announcement while a record is still on the turntable, and this capacity must be taken into account.

What then? Does the radio programme continue as if nothing has happened, until the order arrives to make a public announcement? Or is the announcement made immediately? Or is the station shut down? These questions are for the plotters themselves to answer in the light of local circumstances; all three options present their own obvious risks, the major one being that some untimely warning of what is happening may be obvious from a sudden change in the programme or its sudden disappearance from the air waves. The answer is probably to shut down as many stations as possible (or prevent them from going on the air in the morning) and to use one TV and one radio station to broadcast to the nation. It may be worthwhile bearing in mind, however, that few people will be listening to the radio at night and many of them will probably be less than alert and, unless expecting trouble, will probably put a sudden disappearance from the air waves down to technical 'gremlins'. Besides, a sudden absence of radio programmes tells the listener nothing: it will merely add to the confusion. The real danger arises from an audible disturbance in the studio.

Your next Intelligence Requirement is to find as many people as possible within these media who can assist in the running of the stations and the presentation of your message, and to subvert them in sufficient time to make any changes in their working schedules that are necessary to ensure they are available to assist you.

• **Communications:** It is rarely appreciated just how much a complex machine such as a government relies upon easy, direct communication between its dispersed departments, or how much society as a whole depends on the rapid exchange of information in order to function effectively. Mass communications (those outside the media) tend to consist of telephone or telex-related systems enabling people to speak or send written documents to one another. Your Intelligence Requirement, which is related to your choice of Priority A, B and C targets, is first to discover upon what means of communication they most rely, then to find out from where these communications systems can be controlled.

In the civilian sector we are talking about telephone and telex centres – exchanges, major junctions, nodal centres controlling whole regions. You must understand something of the technology involved, and this becomes very much the responsibility of a technically-minded plotter – ideally a signals expert or a sympathetic communications engineer.

You need to know then the location and nature of the links between your targets and these communications systems and how they may be severed. Finally, you need to know how your area targets – the capital, the regional centres – can be isolated from the rest of the country and the country, in turn, isolated temporarily from the rest of the world.

As with your other targets you need to know locations, manning levels at different times of day and night and at weekends or on holidays, the existence of windows of vulnerability and of sympathetic civilian or military experts who can short-circuit the system on the day of the coup simply by being available to carry out the plotters' orders with regard to the communications infrastructure.

• **Military and government communications:** One way for a government or the armed forces to reduce their vulnerability to coups d'état or sabotage by an enemy is to maintain a parallel system of communications outside the sphere of civilian networks. This is

4. A Typical National Communications Network

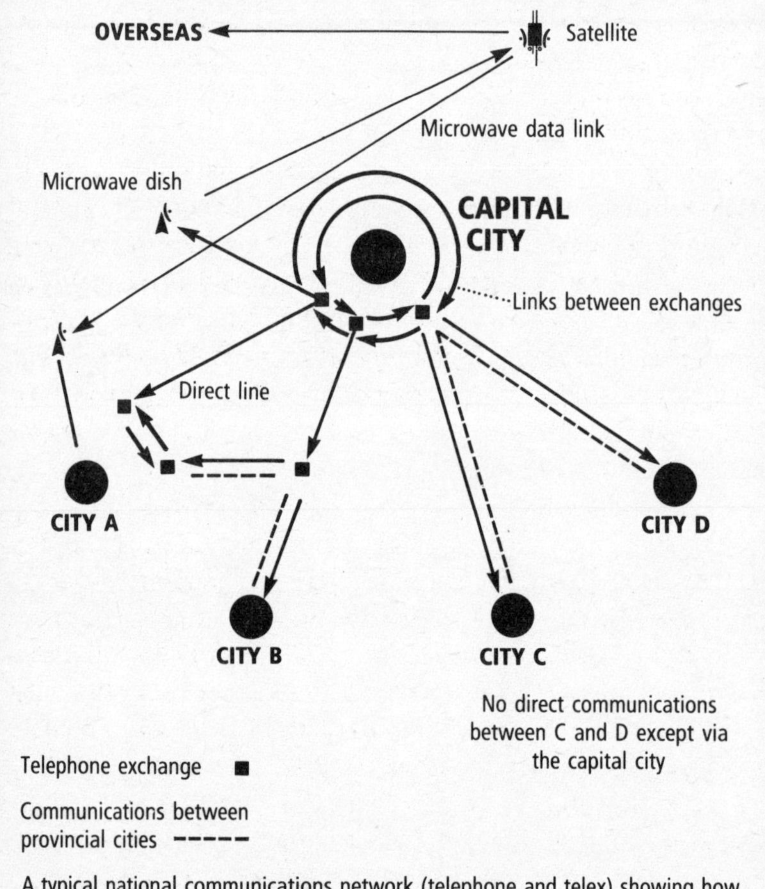

A typical national communications network (telephone and telex) showing how cities speak to each other. Newspapers and news agencies will tend, except in the wealthiest and most advanced countries, to use these facilities as well. The value of good technical Intelligence, which details potential communications 'choke points' for the plotter, can never be overstated.

sound common sense, but presents the plotter with a particular problem, unless he is in a position to exercise direct control over it.

The Intelligence Requirement here is to build up a 'Communications Order of Battle' for both government and military systems (if they are separate). Senior military officers among the plotters will be able to do this quite easily for the military network; subverted civil servants or government ministers (if any exist) will be able to furnish some of the details for the government network; ideally a government technician would fill in the blanks, allowing the plotters to work out which centres must be seized from the very start if the opposition is to be fragmented.

As we are still working to a 'worst case' scenario it is necessary to assume that certain major regional military headquarters will not be subverted and may represent a threat to the success of the plot. These centres must be identified and a conventional military Order of Battle (ORBAT) must be drawn up onto which can be overlaid the Communications ORBAT; this enables you to identify in turn the channels of communication along which orders to act will be passed, from Supreme Headquarters to regional headquarters, to specific formation and unit headquarters.

You must also make absolutely sure that, in each area, you are dealing with a peacetime army (if it is indeed peacetime) so that the right channels are blocked. The United Kingdom provides an interesting example of this distinction: specific units at battalion level or lower tend to receive their orders from either the headquarters of their parent regiment (for administrative purposes) or from regional commands, such as HQ South-East District, for operational purposes. HQ South-East District receives its orders from HQ UK Land Forces, which receives its own orders from the Chief of the General Staff at the Ministry of Defence. In Northern Ireland, however, or in wartime, orders go to the highest formation on the ground and are transmitted down from there; thus the 2nd Battalion, The Parachute Regiment, which might receive its orders directly from HQ SE District at Aldershot during peacetime, bypassing other formation headquarters, would receive orders in wartime from its parent formation,

5. Command Structures and Communications

Typical army command structure and communications ORBAT. In peacetime, note the customary directness of communications between Regional Command and individual units, and also how parallel, but separate, communications systems can be used. While there may be two civilian telephone exchanges between the Ministry of Defence and a distant battalion or regiment there could, ironically enough, be twice as many interfaces (offering twice as much scope for subversion or interdiction of hostile communications) between these same levels using the military network. In wartime the command structure becomes more linear, and direct contact between Unit and Regional Command becomes very much the exception to the rule. Note how a different communications network has replaced the civilian one, although the military network may remain intact. In wartime, it would seem, de-coupling the major elements of an army would be easier than in peacetime (in mechanical terms, at least); security around the various interfaces between communications networks would, of course, be far tighter.

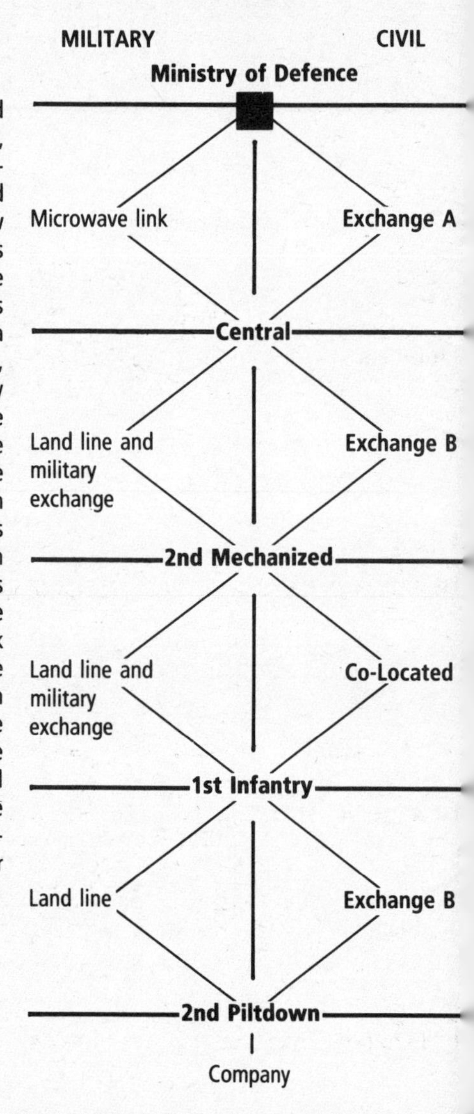

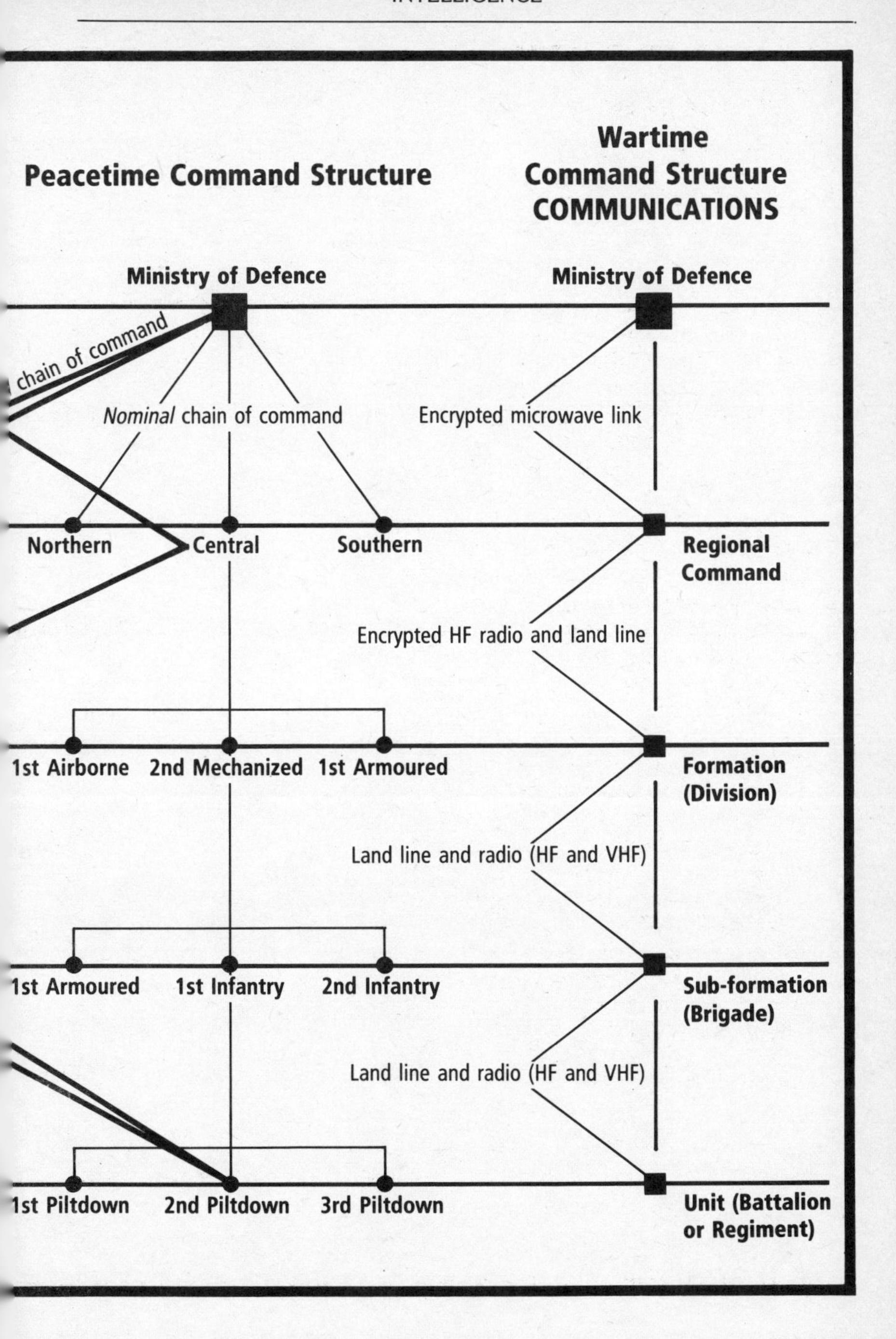
Peacetime Command Structure
Wartime
Command Structure
COMMUNICATIONS
Ministry of Defence
chain of command
Nominal chain of command
Ministry of Defence
Encrypted microwave link
Northern
Central
Southern
Regional
Command
Encrypted HF radio and land line
1st Airborne
2nd Mechanized
1st Armoured
Formation
(Division)
Land line and radio (HF and VHF)
1st Armoured
1st Infantry
2nd Infantry
Sub-formation
(Brigade)
Land line and radio (HF and VHF)
1st Piltdown
2nd Piltdown
3rd Piltdown
Unit (Battalion
or Regiment)

6. The Geographical Subversion Pattern

Range from capital

10km

Bn A (infantry)	**Bn B (infantry)**	**Bn C (infantry)**

50km

Bn D (tank regiment)
7 hours

100km

Bn E (Airmobile)	**Bn F (infantry)**	**Bn G (armoured)**
5 hours	6+ hours	8+ hours

500km

Bn H (parachute)	**Bn I (infantry)**	**Bn J (tank regiment)**
5+ hours	14+ hours	16+ hours

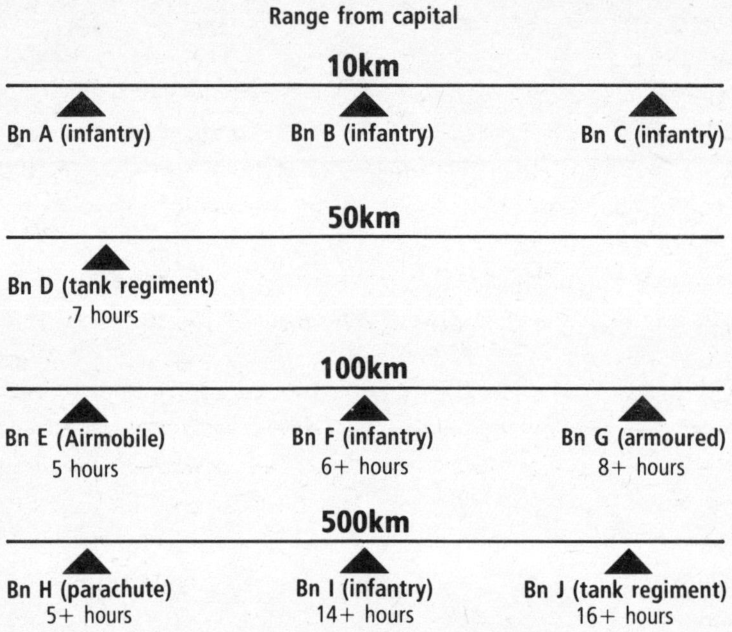

Orders and administration: 2 hours
Draw ammunition and fuel: 2 hours (infantry)
4 hours (armour)
Speed of travel in convoy on good roads: 50kph

The Geographical Subversion Pattern shown here is based on 'best timings': 2 hours to assemble troops and give orders; 2 or 4 hours to issue weapons, fuel and ammunition; and an average speed for most units driving in convoy over anything less than good roads of some 25km/hr. Thus, if the critical Assault and Continuation Phases of the coup are timed to last no longer than 6 hours, by which time the country as a whole and the rest of the armed forces in particular will have been presented with a fait accompli which they have no option but to accept, then it is necessary to subvert or neutralize only battalions A, C, E and H. The others could not react in time to prevent the coup reaching its conclusion. We have not taken into account, of course, the need to 'take out' provincial cities. This would confuse the diagram unnecessarily, but the same rules of distance and speed of reaction would, naturally, feature in any appreciation of the wider problem.

5th Airborne Brigade. In Northern Ireland it would receive its orders from the General Officer Commanding Northern Ireland, through the particular brigade of which it was operationally a member for the duration of its tour of the province.

What you need to know, therefore, is the reporting system used throughout the different regions and the directness of communication between the ministry of defence or army headquarters and individual units or formations in a position to intervene in the coup. Once you know this, you can begin to de-couple the whole.

• **Military facilities:** For 'Military Facilities' read also 'Military formations and units'. As discussed earlier, it may be necessary either to gain control of ordnance depots or to neutralize or subvert units and formations in a position to oppose the coup. The major Intelligence Requirement here has been covered already in 'Manpower and Firepower'; finding out who is available to assist in the coup attempt. Secondary (but no less important) Intelligence Requirements concern the ability or willingness of uncommitted troops to intervene. Much work may be saved by looking at the communications and military ORBATS and, bearing in mind the channels of communication in use throughout the armed forces, considering whether key commanders at regional or command level are likely to be sympathetic to the coup. If so, they can be approached and tasked with keeping 'their' men out of the way while 'your' men get on with the job. Meanwhile, they could assist also in the provision of combat supplies if necessary.

If they are likely to be hostile, the problem becomes one of working out their capacity for intervention and how best to emasculate it. Distant, regional formations are in no position to affect what happens in the capital; regional formations and headquarters closer to the scene of the action could intervene more easily, possibly before the Assault and Continuation Phases of the coup are complete. Communications to the latter should be examined critically (see above), but so should their ORBATS and the physical dispositions of their component parts: it may be found that an entire brigade is dependent upon just one ordnance field park or transport squadron for fuel or vehicles. If these key units can be neutralized, the rest of the formation is crippled, especially if public transport to and from the capital is shut down.

A key phrase used earlier in this book is 'temporary impotence'. The imposition of this state on a unit does not necessarily mean its neutralization; remember that a unit that knows what is going on may be in no position to affect the course of events simply because it is too far away from the action to do anything about it in time to be of any use to the government. If the plotters' judgement of the state of mind of those units which they believe to be uncommitted is correct, sheer physical remoteness may incline their officers and men to do nothing at all, and to sit out the coup with their structure and *esprit de corps* intact. Other units that may wish to oppose the coup, but are too far away to have any effect on its immediate outcome, may be ignored for the time being, especially if defences around the capital have been prepared properly. Later on they can be confronted or, better still, persuaded to acquiesce with the plotters' aims.

The demographics of these units and formations must be considered as well; a coup by, for example, a Christian clique in a mixed Muslim-Christian country may provoke a backlash from Muslims in the armed forces. The likelihood of this must be weighed and taken into account. A detailed Intelligence picture should also be built up, if possible, of the state of mind of these units: the feelings of the officers must be weighed and considered and so, crucially, should those of the NCOs and troops. There is no sense in being Utopian at this stage – if there is any likelihood that officers and other ranks may disagree violently over what is happening, it is as well to know, for better or worse, which side will come out on top and who they will support.

This problem arose in the French Army in Algeria during the Generals' *putsch* of 21 April 1961. While the paratroopers and their officers were, on the wholie, firmly behind the *putsch*ists, the conscripts and some of their officers weren't, being in Algeria pretty much against their will and being disinclined also to stick their necks out for an army they hadn't really wanted to join in the first place.

General Challe, the ringleader in the coup, failed to take into account the apathy of the conscripts and some of the other branches of the armed forces in Algiers (surprisingly, since he was an air force General) and the coup failed due, basically, to the lack of momentum which greater numbers of troops might have lent to the *Algérie Française* movement of which Challe was *de facto* commander.

In more specific terms you need to know the location of every component of formations or units in a position to intervene – as well as their composition – and where they keep their vehicles, weapons and ammunition; you need to know how these can be sabotaged or neutralized; whether any of the officers or NCOs there may be able and willing to help you without fear of reprisals from their fellows. Finally, you need to know how they would get from their forming-up areas and assembly points to the capital or regional centre in question so that, if the worst comes to the worst, they can be confronted by visible proof of the plotters' determination to carry out the coup. One advantage of carrying out a thorough appreciation of the military communications ORBAT is that you should be in a position to know exactly how much they know about what is going on and, therefore, how much you may be able to bluff about your own strength and popularity.

• **Levers of power:** We seem to have covered most of the obvious levers of real (not necessarily political) power in the preceding pages; but there may be other factors peculiar to a specific country or set of circumstances of which you are unaware. A coup d'état is a political act and its objectives are all political in nature. It is, therefore, vital to keep a finger on the political pulse of the nation. With the best will in the world a professional serviceman, especially a senior officer, cannot help but be politically aware. He may not be so aware that he is intimately acquainted with the ins and outs of political life within his own country, but he is sure to know senior political figures with whom he shares a mutual respect. These figures will probably know their way around the labyrinth of a modern state's political and constitutional apparatus and will be able to furnish invaluable Intelligence and background information on some of the targets, as well as assisting in selecting the best time to strike and some of the priorities, if these happen to change during the planning process.

It must not be forgotten that a coup d'état is not a purely military manoeuvre; it is a political act carried out using force of arms. While certain critical military factors must be taken into account where planning and execution are concerned, the political objectives should not be compromised on the altar of military expediency or dogma. War is too serious a business to be left to Generals, wrote one political animal; he might have said the same about coups d'état. On the other hand, the plotters (including the military) should bear in mind one vital piece of military theory: Selection and Maintenance of Aim. A coup is not an exercise in the misuse of military power, it is an exercise in the seizure of political power. Purely military considerations should not be allowed unduly to disturb the aim of the politicians among the plotters, but nor should sound military principles be sacrified on the altar of politics to the detriment of the coup's chances of success.

One factor other than Intelligence should be borne in mind at this stage – timings. The subject will be dealt with in more detail later on, but it is important to build them into the Intelligence Requirement. The requirement in this case is to work out what is the best time overall to carry out the coup itself, bearing in mind all the various factors which have had to be integrated into the coup plan.

It is a standing joke among NATO troops that if the Russians want to invade Europe they should do so either at Easter or on either Boxing Day or New Year's Day, when the majority of NATO soldiers (especially the Scottish and some Germans) will be generating or suffering from enormous hangovers, either in barracks or back home on leave. The same applies to your coup plot. When are all the conditions right for you to move? It should be at night, this we know already, but which night? The eve of the Sabbath may be a good time, or the Sabbath itself, or a public holiday when the streets are empty and most of the government's infrastructure is manned by skeleton staffs.

You need to know where the windows of vulnerability coincide to your greatest advantage across a broad range of targets, which means doing a little lateral thinking (in military terms, at least) so that the strike doesn't take place at a highly embarrassing time, such as during the state visit of a friendly head of state or during one of the local rounds of soccer's World Cup, when the country will be full of foreign pressmen and camera and radio crews.

We shall look at this particular Intelligence Requirement in the next Chapter, but the point must be made here that this aspect of the timings must be considered from the very start so that last-minute changes of plan (which are almost inevitable, even in the best-run operations) are kept to a minimum.

One final Intelligence Requirement concerns the 'sponsoring' states mentioned earlier. You need to know exactly what is likely to happen should the complexion of our present government change unexpectedly (which is what you are trying to make happen). Will the Russians invade? Or their Cuban surrogates? Will the Americans invade instead? Or start supporting opposition groups as they are doing at present in Nicaragua? Will the British or French suddenly withdraw their military assistance teams or impose an oil or arms or trade embargo on you? Or will they suddenly recognize a new ally and pour cash, commodities and arms into the country to speed it on its new course?

The last people to whom one should put these questions are the diplomats at the embassies concerned, or the known agents of these countries' Intelligence agencies. If, for some reason, they report back to the government, the plotters are in trouble. And if the plotters pose a threat to a cosy relationship between the foreign power and your own country these diplomats and agents may be only too glad to spoil the operation. In many cases it will be only too obvious who one's ideological enemies are so, while avoiding the American Intelligence-gathering agencies, one could try to canvas support from the Soviet Union, or vice versa.

The problem to be borne in mind here, of course, is the old one of political favours. Assistance from one power or another makes one beholden to that power and vulnerable to requests – or demands – for favours in return, or simply to an undue amount of influence from one's new 'friends'. Unless there is a particular ideological bias in any one direction, or a particular need for assistance of a specific kind, there is a very good argument to be made for avoiding outside agencies as far as possible. On the home front, if nowhere else, there is much to be said for a totally 'homegrown' coup d'état which owes nothing to an outside agency and which bears the stamp of authenticity in ethnic, religious or regional terms.

6
MEANS
The Mechanics of Planning

In the previous Chapter we dealt with the problem of Intelligence as it relates to the planners of a coup d'état. This Chapter deals with some of the more mundane problems of planning a coup, not least that of doing so without being caught in the act. It is probably fair to say that the more senior in either political or military rank the planner is, the easier his job becomes. Not only does information come more easily to hand, but he can give orders without too many of them being questioned by his subordinates and the less the likelihood of somebody above breathing down the planner's neck to see what he is doing.

The plot to kill Hitler in July 1944 provides perhaps the best example of this. The July Plot was an audacious attempt to pull off a coup d'état in a country gone rotten and which was now facing defeat on two fronts. Without going into it in any depth, suffice to say that it was created by some of the senior Generals in the Wehrmacht Home Command in Berlin and allowed to mature over many months. The whole plot hinged on the sense of duty of lower-ranking German officers and men; very few of them disobeyed orders so it was necessary only for a few Generals to put the plan together themselves and then, come *Der Tag*, simply tell the troops under their command what to do. The rest would fall into place. The plan backfired, through a combination of bad luck and the inherent unwillingness of German officers to enter into intrigues. What is important is that the Operations Order, Plan 'Valkyrie' lay undisturbed in a General's filing cabinet for months, quietly maturing, and labelled 'Scheme for Defending Berlin from Air Attack'. Nobody searched the officer's filing cabinet until after his arrest on Hitler's orders.

Compare the experience of these Generals with that of the Commanding Officer of the 2nd Armoured Regiment of the Chilean Army in June 1973. Not only was his plot discovered, but he was publicly humiliated and his career ruined; he had no means of protecting his plot from the Chilean security service. Remember that it was a junior officer, a captain, who was arrested initially. Was this officer 'fingered' by some security service infiltrator in the regiment? Or had the security services infiltrated the Patria y Libertad National Front, the officers' co-conspirators? We may never known, but it is not important. The important thing to bear in mind here is the physical problem of planning a coup, one which will succeed and one which will not be compromised before it is put into operation.

Seen from the point of view of the military alone, there should not be too many problems so long as the planners are of a high enough rank. Except in the most unstable countries, run by paranoid heads of state such as Idi Amin or Hitler, senior personnel tend to command the respect and trust of both security services and government. They are rarely subject to petty restrictions or more than routine investigations; to this level of trust must be added the fact that the military world is essentially a closed one, almost monastic in its particular form of isolation from the mainstream of civilian life. Thus very few outside the barrack gates will question what goes on inside – they wouldn't understand half of what goes on in any case.

MODELS OF CONSPIRACY

Depending upon the military rank of the conspirators and the level of contact they have with civilian partners, there are a number of Models of Conspiracy, each more or less appropriate to the type of plot in question and to which the majority of coups d'état have conformed. The first is the most obvious one, typified by Chile in 1973, Germany in 1944, and Nigeria on New Year's Eve 1983: a coup mounted almost entirely by the military and planned at the very top. In this case the isolation of the military from civilian life allows the plot to develop unhindered with only the few most senior officers involved in planning and co-ordination. Come the glorious day they have only to use the armed forces' existing and well-tried system of communications to pass on their orders to lower command echelons and the plot will proceed.

The second Model of Conspiracy supposes a combined civilian-military plot involving the most senior military officers and elements of the government or opposition parties in an attempt to overthrow an unpopular head of state and/or the ruling party, replacing them with either civilian or civil-military rulers.

The third Model is still fairly unusual, although by now well-defined: a coup mounted from outside the country by mercenaries or irregular or foreign troops, perhaps working with disaffected civilian opposition elements in-country.

The fourth Model is the *putsch*, a coup planned and mounted by a clique within the armed forces, and not necessarily a senior clique, either. Each of these four models of conspiracy represents a particular combination of tensions and dissatisfactions within the country and its armed forces, and different motivations on the parts of the plotters. The planning problems each model represents are a reflection (in the very broadest terms only, of course) of the likelihood of the coup's success. For example, the second model, while suggesting deep civilian disaffection with the current government and a willingness to join forces with the military in overthrowing it, may be extremely vulnerable to infiltration by the government's security services, especially if the conspirators are known dissidents. The fourth model, if planned by the wrong sort of clique (a minority tribe in an army dominated by one large tribal group, for example), may be vulnerable to the army's own security agencies and to a sharp response by the rest of the service, under the command of senior loyal officers.

The 'safest' model is the first, in which the armed forces (or perhaps only one of the services) operates in a self-contained manner, drawing upon its own resources for Intelligence, Firepower, Manpower and Planning. Even this model is vulnerable, however; a self-contained, almost inward-looking institution may not be in any position to make a valid judgement of the state of mind of the nation, nor to avoid some elementary political mistakes which a more overtly politicized plotter, closer to the roots of the society in which he lives, might spot in advance.

Much will depend, naturally, on the morbidity of the servicemen themselves, their tendency towards a narrow view of the world in general and local conditions in particular. In the case of the second and third models we have to assume that liaison between civilians and military is sufficient to lend political direction to the military operation and no more; close day-to-day contact, while desirable from the planning point of view, may be an unacceptable security risk, to say nothing of being extremely difficult in the case of a mercenary operation.

Let us look at some of these models in more detail.

• **Model Number One:** Where the planning of the coup is being carried out at the highest level within the armed forces, the entire Intelligence-gathering, planning and military resources of the country are, in theory, at the disposal of the plotters. This is not the case in practice, however. To use the full powers of an army or air force commander in order to plan a coup d'état would inevitably arouse suspicion among junior staff officers and commanders of certain active units who may not wish a coup to take place.

Despite this, considerable use can be made of the pool of talent available within the armed forces, Senior commanders in most armies are allowed a certain amount of freedom in selecting their own staff and subordinates, and so can gather around themselves men capable of seeing such a project through from inception to execution. Liaison between commanders and staff officers is aided by the 'Old Boy Network' which exists in all but a very few forces. There is never just one such network, there are usually several and they are stratified to cover their own particular generations. For example, officers of the rank of, say, brigadier and above will, by virtue of attrition rates during the rise up the promotional ladder, tend to be few in number, but acquainted with one another at the very least and, possibly through shared training courses or postings earlier on, good friends. The same applies to more junior officers who may have been through officer training or staff college, or even a campaign, together.

This all means that communication and liaison can be carried out at an informal level with very little being done through the normal channels. These channels, below a certain level, tend to be vertical in their orientation, thus keeping the 1st Armoured Division, for example, quite separate in communications terms from, say, the 2nd Armoured Division. But if the chief of staff of one is a good friend of the chief of staff of the other, even where the two divisional commanders are unknown to each other, liaison can be close, effective and discreet – after all, there are no laws against brother officers meeting socially in one another's homes or during courtesy visits to other units or formations. At a slightly higher level, senior commanders have a positive duty to liaise with one another to ensure the smoother functioning of the armed forces; many of these senior commanders will be good friends – indeed, by virtue of their age and rank, they will probably be old friends and nobody is going to deny an elderly man the pleasures of comradeship and human contact; still less will a junior officer question the right of his superiors to meet whom they like when they like.

If planning meetings take place in barracks, however, there is a danger that somebody will notice when General X begins to spend more of his time at General Y's headquarters than at his own. If that somebody is a police or security service informer, questions might be asked. One advantage of the military's comparative isolation is the fact that in many countries very few senior officers are known to the general public; meetings outside barracks, in private homes or at clubs and restaurants, where the plotters wear civilian clothes, would arouse no suspicion at all. And if junior liaison officers are used intelligently the danger of being compromised is reduced.

The overriding advantage of a coup planned along the lines of this first Model of Conspiracy is that security can be as tight as required, while the 'Old Boy Network' allows opinions to be sounded out throughout the army (or other service) rapidly, informally and discreetly, thus allowing a totally realistic appreciation of the forces available to the plotters to be made at an early stage.

• **Model Number Two:** Collusion between politicians and soldiers is not uncommon in countries where the armed forces are heavily politicized. Nevertheless, such collusion is often forced upon the partners as even like-minded soldiers and politicians acknowledge the basic differences in ethic and viewpoint arising from their separate vocations. The purpose of such collusion is frequently for the soldiers to clear the way for the civilians to take over after the old government has fallen. Such close partnership is frequently Utopian, however, as the military often finds it hard to relinquish the power it has gained once the coup has succeeded. Frequently the disposition on the part of the military to intervene in government is merely a reflection of a growing praetorianism which will not stop at acting as somebody else's blunt instrument.

Assuming that such a partnership exists (and many do, and have done), what are the physical planning problems involved? The first is to arrive at an acceptable accommodation between the civil and the military men; there must exist between them a level of harmony, if not outright trust, which will prevent the onset of bickering and argument whcih may result in regrettable incidents and betrayals arising solely from one party's pique.

Having established a working relationship the next problem is to establish the political aims of the coup and to translate these into military objectives. This stage can be the most dangerous; it requires close liaison between the senior military and civilian planners over what may be an extended period, with several meetings taking place. In a country where the opposition parties, and even members of the ruling party, are known to be disloyal, there is considerable danger that the politicians concerned may be under investigation. Any reasonably astute head of state, on receiving reports of clandestine meetings between, say, the leader of the opposition and his army chief of staff will put two and two together very quickly.

So much is obvious, and probably needs no emphasis here; the point to be made, though, is that liaison is important and cannot be ignored. If necessary, two trusted nominees must be ordered to meet on behalf of their masters, go-betweens who will not arouse suspicion. The real danger is that a civilian is unlikely to be familiar with the basic requirements of security in such a context and so is likely to compromise himself; but it is no part of this book to go into what the spy novelist, John Le Carré, calls 'Tradecraft', and besides the right selection of nominees may render such melodramatic measures unnecessary. The point must be emphasized, however, that security in such a plot is far more important than in our first model.

In a situation where both the military and civilian plotters are revolutionary in complexion – and especially where they hold either minority views or such extreme ones that the government is prepared to take quite far-reaching measures against such people if they are caught doing anything even remotely treasonable – it can be taken as read that the plotters will be the subject of quite stringent surveillance. It is the military plotter who holds the key here; his feelings may be reflected by just one or two units or formations within the armed forces, or by a small but influential minority spread across several units. Whatever the case, he has the dual problems not only of avoiding detection by the security services but also of keeping the plot secret from his superiors while it is maturing. Let us take the case of, say, a clique of middle-ranking officers of about the rank of captain or major who wish to mount a revolutionary coup d'état which will result in the overthrow of the entire Establishment. Such a coup will almost inevitably involve bloodshed, possibly on a large scale and certainly from H-Hour itself. Once begun, such a coup must be carried out to its conclusion – win or die – if the plotters are to count upon both surviving and enjoying their liberty afterwards.

There can be no mistakes in either planning or Intelligence for such a coup; quite apart from the political targets which must be 'taken out', a great deal of thought must be devoted to the problem of preventing any sort of retaliation by loyalist forces and, of course, to assembling the largest possible revolutionary force consistent with the requirements of the plan itself. The twin problems of low rank and tight security may make such a feat seem almost impossible, but it has been done before, notably in countries such as Ghana and Liberia. One problem to watch out for in particular is that of approaching a more senior officer who could either take over some of the planning (if he has a headquarters at his disposal or sufficient experience to put together a workable plan himself), or act as a figurehead during the immediate aftermath of the coup. Not only is there a risk that he will betray the plot, there is an added risk that he may subvert it or 'hijack' it for his own ends; if he sees that a coup is inevitable and does not trust the men who have approached him, or believe their promises concerning his post-coup future, he may decide that the coup is best run by himself for himself – and that the original plotters, once the coup is over, are dispensable.

If the plotters are of low rank it may not be possible to count upon entire units joining the coup. In such a situation the forces available to them will consist of dribs and drabs, individuals from one unit, platoons or companies from another, hastily armed 'militias' drawn from the revolutionary parties, and so on. Entire formations may be untouched by the plot, especially if there are any tribal or ethnic overtones to it. The same applies to the population; the majority may have no stomach for the revolution so they may need to be coerced into accepting it by the presentation of a *fait accompli* and a display of invincible force. Without a doubt, this particular model of conspiracy is the most difficult to follow.

It is probably worth bearing in mind for this model in particular, but for the others as well to a greater or lesser degree, the value of foreign assistance. The coup d'état which overthrew Sultan Said bin Taimur of Oman in July 1970 was typical of this particular model, but could probably not have succeeded without the passive assistance (at the very least) of the British. The Sultan was old, reactionary and a liability both to Oman's development and to the security of the Gulf in general. His son, Qaboos, had been virtually confined to house arrest after his return home from Sandhurst and a short spell with the British Army. Alarmed at what he saw happening to the country he would one day inherit, and increasingly angered by his father's political ineptitude (which was making the Dhofar insurrection in the south of the Sultanate even more difficult to contain), he began to conspire with a small circle of trusted colleagues: his father's secretary; the son of a senior local politician; and a former classmate from Sandhurst, now a member of the Intelligence staff of the Sultan's armed forces (SAF). Using a series of go-betweens, Qaboos was able to put together a plan which received the discreet blessing of those people in the British Foreign and Commonwealth Office who felt that Said's departure would be a good thing.

The FCO's blessing in London was translated into concrete assistance on the ground by the steady removal or rotation of those British officers and personnel serving under contract to the SAF who felt real loyalty towards Said, and their replacement with Qaboos's sympathizers. On 23 July 1970 the plot was put into action and one of Qaboos's lieutenants led a small force of Omanis into the Royal Palace at Salalah where, after a short fire fight, the Sultan was heavily wounded and surrendered. Almost immediately, Qaboos assumed his father's title and powers and a joint British-Omani committee took over the running of the country until Qaboos held the reins of government firmly enough himself.

The Omani example falls somewhere between the first and second models, but only by virtue of the fact that the SAF was staffed largely by British officers for whom British Government permission was necessary before they could become involved (or, more accurately, avoid any real involvement). Remove the British factor from this particular coup and you have a fairly typical, mainstream example of the second model of conspiracy.

• **Model Number Three:** The third model of conspiracy supposes the use of mercenaries of one kind or another, or foreign troops who can carry out the coup without any need to involve local troops – who may be loyal to the government in any case.

Benin, the Seychelles, Grenada and The Comoros have all been cited as examples of this particular model. A number of factors are common to all these coups. The first is a secure jumping-off point for the attackers; the second is extremely close liaison between the attackers, their sponsors (who may be in exile) and supporters on the ground; the third is a very low level of political culture and national infrastructure. In the case of Grenada the jumping-off point was the small offshore island of Carriacou where some of the New Jewel Movement's arms were cached and where the attacking force was based following military training overseas. Nobody is really certain where the arms came from, but it seems they were bought more or less on the open market; there were very few to go around and the assault teams relied for success more on speed and surprise than firepower. Besides, once the armouries of the tiny Grenadian Army and police force had been captured, there was no shortage of arms available for the New Jewel Movement's supporters.

Like the Grenada operation, Albert René's takeover of the Seychelles relied less upon firepower than surprise. Sixty men assembled on one of the outlying islands and, when President Mancham was absent at the Commonwealth Leader's Conference in London, they flew into the main island, Mahé. There, armed with just 20 rifles (supplied, it is alleged, by the Tanzanians), they stormed the armoury at Montfleury police barracks which contained the only weapons of any kind on the island. It was all over in a matter of minutes.

Both of these coups were characterized by the fact that the new heads of state were already on the ground, but living and working in a political environment where violence on this sort of scale was unheard of and therefore not prepared for. Security was a major consideration in the planning of these coups, naturally, but there was, in general, so little suspicion that planning went ahead unmolested; René's and Bishop's intermediaries were able to come and go, and to plot and plan, pretty much as they pleased.

The same was not true of either Denard's coup in Benin or Hoare's coup in the Seychelles. For a start, both prospective heads of states were in exile: Jimmy Mancham in London and Dr Emile Zanzou in Côte d'Ivoire. Let us look at Hoare's problems first.

The great advantage that Hoare enjoyed was the sizeable community of expatriate Seychellois living in South Africa (where he was based), London and Australia, and their highly developed sense of organization. The *Mouvement pour la Résistance*, an underground movement to which many of these exiles belonged, had branches in all of these places and a comparatively large organization on the ground in the Seychelles. Communications between Hoare and Mancham or the latter's lieutenants was no problem, and there were enough secret members of the *Mouvement* for information to travel freely between the Seychelles and either London or Hoare's home at Pietermaritzburg.

Secondly, Hoare had the tacit approval of the South African National Intelligence Service (NIS) in this venture. One of their operatives, Martin Dolinchek, assisted in the planning of the operation and acted as liaison officer between Hoare and the NIS deputy chief, N.I. Classen. Even more astonishingly, Kenya was prepared to assist Hoare, Mancham, the Seychellois militants-in-exile and the South Africans in getting rid of an annoying and possibly threatening Tanzanian presence just off its coast. Hoare's only problem was to raise the money – the South Africans supplied the weapons, some of the Seychellois supplied some of the Intelligence, and Martin Dolinchek and Hoare undertook their own 'recces' of the islands before going firm on their plans. Mercenaries were easily found: former Rhodesian soldiers from the Selous Scouts, Rhodesian Light Infantry and SAS, leavened with a number of British and Europeans, and stiffened by a few members of the South African Citizen Force were all it would take to overthrow René's government – about 45 men in all.

In retrospect, Hoare seems to have had a remarkably easy time because the only people he had to keep his secret from were the PUP Government on the island; everybody was determined to help with everything except money. Kenya agreed to allow Mancham to use the country as a jumping-off point for his own return to the Islands while Hoare and his men would fly in disguised as a rugby football team on a Royal Air Swazi scheduled flight taking off from Matsapa Airport in

Swaziland. Only the unbelievable stupidity of one South African mercenary brought about the disastrous failure of the coup attempt. Hoare planned the operation down to the very last detail and there is absolutely no doubt in my mind that the operation would have been successful had it been allowed the chance to go ahead.

Denard's problems in Benin were of an entirely different nature. As in all operations of this kind he had to have a safe jumping-off point which, in fact, he had in Franceville, Gabon. A friendly country abutting on the target was necessary – in this case Togo, whose Head of State, President Eyadema, was frightened of Benin's expansionist plans. Without a doubt the French Government assisted Denard wherever they could without becoming directly involved. They must have brought some influence to bear so that President Eyadema and President Bongo of Gabon could liaise directly, while securing the assistance of King Hassan of Morocco in providing training facilities for the mercenaries. It is not clear where Denard or the other principals got their Intelligence from. Certainly both Zinzou and his liaison officer with Denard, an ex-ambassador named Gratien Pognon, had both served under Kerekou in the Benin Government, but it is not clear whether there was anybody on the ground within Cotonou itself who could update Denard on the operational situation inside the city.

It seems that much of the Intelligence-gathering, apart from a brief recce carried out by Denard himself, was done from outside the country's borders. This would seem to be borne out by the fact that there was no organization on the ground that could supply guides or assistants for the attacking force. As mentioned earlier there was a major Intelligence failure (a stroke of bad luck, really, but one for which Denard should have allowed) and this coup attempt, as well, was a failure.

The lessons to be drawn from these examples are these. If mounting a mercenary-type coup from within the target country's own borders, a certain level of political *naïveté* on the part of the target government is vital if the coup is to have any hope of success. Whether a coup is planned from within the country or from offshore, the country and its infrastructure must be compact and simple enough for a small unit to seize control of it in a matter of hours. If planning and mounting the coup from overseas, the active co-operation of at least one neighbouring state is vital to provide both a jumping-off point and back-up forces if required; also so that planning can be carried out in peace and quiet with the minimum risk of discovery by the target country. Finally, there must be a clandestine organization within the target country which can provide Intelligence and any back-up services needed during the coup itself and immediately afterwards – even Frederick Forsyth's mercenaries in *The Dogs of War* enjoyed this support in the form of a colony of immigrants.

• **Model Number Four:** In some ways, this final model – the *putsch* – is the trickiest of all. A *putsch* is traditionally carried out by a clique within the armed forces, and relies on no outside support at all from either politicians or external agencies. The July Plot to kill Hitler was a *putsch*, but one confounded not only by the institutional ineptitude of highly professional Wehrmacht officers trying to be plotters, but also by the fact that other troops in the Berlin areas included Waffen-SS and Luftwaffe Fallschirmjägern, none of whom felt any particular loyalty to Wehrmacht officers other then their own.

The best recent example of a *putsch* is the 1961 Algiers coup carried out by Generals Salan, Challe, Zeller and Jouhaud. This *putsch* failed as well, and for much the same reasons as the July Plot, but with one conspicuous difference: instead of carrying it out in the capital, as the Wehrmacht Generals did, the Frenchmen carried out theirs in Algiers, some 1,500 miles from Paris where the major decisions regarding Algeria's future were being taken.

In retrospect, it seems that the intended victims of the *putsch*, President De Gaulle and Prime Minister Debré, knew more about the planning of coups d'état than the four Generals; from the very first announcement of the coup on Algiers Radio they had daily expected 'les Paras' to float down from the sky over Paris and overthrow the Fifth Republic. No paratroopers appeared, however, and the *putsch* itself lasted barely five days. Why? First of all, and most importantly, the Generals were not capable of forming a government themselves, and seem to have made no attempt to do so – in effect, nothing changed in Algeria. Secondly, because they had apparently gained no moral ascendancy over either the French conscipts in Algeria or the government in Paris who had sent them there, the conscripts (or, rather, the officers in those line regiments staffed mainly by conscripts) did not join the *putsch*. Thirdly, the various right-wing factions which supported the Generals were fragmented, and the plotters did nothing to bring them together – indeed, it was *France Résistance* (FR) activists who were invited to play the major part in the coup itself rather than the larger, better-organized and more militant *Organisation Armée Secrète* (OAS). This did not endear the plotters to many people.

Finally, the plot simply lost momentum. There was no Government in Algiers to be overthrown, so there was no new dawn in French and Algerian affairs; simply a rebellious outburst, removed from the centre of power, which achieved nothing and was soon over. The Generals' political judgement had been quite non-existent.

In one area alone was the Generals' *putsch* a qualified success – that of operational planning. Much of this was done in Paris, where the French secret service was less of a threat than in Algiers; more still was done in Madrid. Very little seems to have been done, at least in military terms, in Algeria itself. It is interesting to note that the strongest feelings on the issue of Algérie Française were held by the right-wing militant groups such as the OAS and FR, the former of which later became a rather odious terrorist organization, and by a minority of the French Army, Navy and Air Force. The *pieds noirs* population of Algeria was in the minority and only a proportion of them actively supported the militants. Thus co-ordinating instructions between the army conspirators and the militants could be passed quite easily, especially as some of the latter were themselves ex-paratroopers who had remained in Algeria and who had maintained contact with their old regiments, especially the 1er REP (*Régiment Etranger Parachutiste*) at its barracks in Zeralda, some 30 miles outside Algiers.

There existed one major threat to the conspirators – the climate of intrigue prevalent in Algeria during late 1960 and early 1961. The French police and security services had finely tuned antennae and could pick up a great deal of information from infiltrators and informants; on the other hand, so much was happening that they were frequently over-stretched. Besides, if it had been made known that officers in the French Army – especially senior and revered Generals such as Salan – were involved in a plot of these dimensions, and if they had been arrested, there is no telling what divisive effects such a move would have had on the army. Having said that, of course, it was known in France that a number of senior and middle-ranking officers were plotting, but nobody knew what the plot involved or when it would culminate. A number of planning meetings in Paris were observed (some were even infiltrated by the security services) and, as soon as Prime Minister Michel Debré received word from Algiers that the coup had taken place, he was able to give orders for those plotters remaining in Paris to be detained immediately.

7
EXECUTION
Preparation for Battle

In discussing the problems of planning a coup, and the objective which the plotters must achieve before there can be said to be a worthwhile plan (as opposed to a plot, which is not the same thing at all), we have not referred to the means by which the entire edifice is given the initial jolt which sets it rolling towards its conclusion. Once the plan exists in terms of targets and agencies available to 'take them out', two points remain to be finalized: the date of the strike and the means of mobilizing the forces taking part.

It is quite possible that a date exists on which the coup not only can take place but *must* do so, for no matter what reason; but it is more likely that the date will be set some time after planning has commenced. Once reason for this is that, while windows of vulnerability with regard to certain targets are known to exist from time to time (and one is concerned here especially with certain human targets), it is not always possible to identify these a long time in advance. Once they have been identified, of course, it will almost certainly become necessary to alter certain elements of the plan to accommodate them, but its basic structure should be kept intact if possible.

It was stated before that the astute plotter will time the coup so as to avoid, say, visiting dignitaries or heads of state, or the presence of the foreign Press during an international football match or public event. A coup can also be timed to coincide with the head of state's absence from the country: Milton Obote, Sir Eric Gairy, James

Mancham and Major-General Yakubu Gowon are all heads of state whose countries have changed hands during their absence (all, with the exception of Gairy, at either OAU or Commonwealth Heads of State conferences – food for thought there!). The absence of the major human target makes a coup d'état somewhat easier to carry through because he is unable to exert any personal influence over what happens during the coup itself, and also because, for the first vital few hours, he has no idea what is happening at home. He will usually learn from his host that he is no longer head of state, that his power base at home no longer exists and that he has no machinery to hand by which he can wrest power back from the usurpers.

If the coup can be carried out in this way the chances of blood being shed are far less than if the head of state is present to co-ordinate resistance and confront the plotters with loyalist forces. It makes sense, therefore, to plan a coup with just such an absence in mind. If, however, an emergency summit meeting is called at short notice to which the head of state must travel overseas, such an opportunity should not be allowed to pass, so long as the planning is sufficiently flexible to permit a sudden change in schedule.

It must be borne in mind, of course, that one doesn't make sudden changes that will necessitate a fundamental change in plan; if the original plan called for a coup to take place on a Saturday night because this was when most of the population stayed at home, it would be stupid to mount the coup on a different night when bars, cafes and restaurants were open until two or three in the morning and the city centre remained busy until dawn.

TIMING

The ideal situation for the plotter is a date, known well in advance, when the head of state is either absent from the country or extremely vulnerable, and which coincides with what is certain to be a quiet night in the city and provinces. Theory and practice rarely go hand in hand, however, so such a windfall must not be counted on. It is significant that the attempted Seychelles coup of 1981 was timed to coincide not only with President René's absence from the islands but also a cabinet meeting at which the majority of human targets would be present – packaged, if you like, for abduction. In the UK one might consider mounting a coup during the State Opening of Parliament when almost the entire Establishment would be present in the Palace of Westminster; if the intention was the removal of the politicians without harming either the monarch or the institution of monarchy, one might instead wait until the opening day of a new parliamentary session – one could 'take out' peers and MPs in one fell swoop. Of course, one would then be faced with the problem of sabotaging the BBC and independent broadcasting facilities at Westminster, just in case some regrettable incident was either broadcast live or recorded – to be used in evidence in the future, as happened in the abortive Spanish coup of 1975.

One thing which the wise plotter does not attempt is a coup d'état timed for the head of state's visit to one of his regional power bases. In Zimbabwe, for example, anybody trying to overthrow a head of state or prime minister from, say, the Mashona tribe (especially if the plotter were a Matabele) would not do so when the figure concerned was addressing a party rally deep in his own tribal area. The prospect of the entire Mashona nation mobilizing to restore a leader capable of commanding their obedience and motivating them sufficiently to take direct action is not one to be considered with equanimity.

Interestingly enough, Rhodesia (later Zimbabwe) has never seen a coup d'état although, to my knowledge, two have been planned which could have altered the course of the country's history enormously. The first was planned – and then cancelled – in 1964, shortly before the Smith regime made its Unilateral Declaration of Independence. The dynamics of this particular coup are interesting. Ian Smith was not universally popular in Rhodesia and General Peter Walls was not the most popular or respected man in the Rhodesian Army, but they managed, between them, to bring the country round and pursue its own path towards independence.

It had been known for some time before Smith made his announcement that something serious was going to happen, and few in Rhodesia had any doubts what it would be. According to one participant, it was decided that Smith could not be allowed to go ahead with what he was planning. The participant, who had once been a comparatively senior officer in C Squadron, 22 SAS (the Rhodesian unit raised to fight alongside British SAS squadrons in Malaya), was asked quietly by a senior member of the British Colonial Administration if Smith (and possibly Walls as well) could be 'taken out'. A plan was drawn up and presented to the senior official who then asked whether the officer could guarantee that there would be no bloodshed. The officer naturally gave no such guarantee and the idea was dropped. A month later Smith made his declaration. Peter Walls had promised him the unqualified support of the Rhodesian Army and had manoeuvred himself into a situation where the army had either to follow Walls' orders or be riven by internal dissent and mutiny – anathema to what was, at the time, one of the most professional armies in Africa.

The British never had another opportunity to end UDI peacefully – the deployment of squadrons of RAF fighters and bombers and thousands of men to East Africa to prepare for an invasion of Rhodesia was simply an exercise in slamming the stable door after the horse had bolted. A timely coup d'état in 1964, which a majority of Rhodesians might have accepted then, especially as the country was still a more or less loyal colony, might have saved 40,000 lives in the bush war which followed, and would certainly have altered the colour of the current political map of Southern Africa.

The second coup was planned just before Zimbabwe (as the country is now known) received its formal independence in 1980. According to a member of the regiment who subsequently left the country, the Rhodesian Light Infantry (RLI), one of the élite formations in a highly professional army, and one of the best counter-insurgency units in the world, was 'wired up' ready to overthrow the new government of Prime Minister Robert Mugabe before it could be installed formally. Only one thing, it seemed, prevented the coup from going ahead; the presence in Zimbabwe of a Commonwealth Force to monitor the ceasefire and keep a watchful eye on both the black ex-guerrillas and the still tense Rhodesian Army. A sudden flaring of violence by the RLI would have enraged the guerrillas and, more importantly one suspects, resulted in the Commonwealth troops opening fire on the white rebels in order to demonstrate their good faith to the blacks. Besides, there were now some 30,000 guerrillas, all armed, concentrated in camps around the main centres of Zimbabwe. The RLI alone could not have defended Salisbury (now Harare) against such numbers, far less won this new war.

There would never have been a good time for this coup to take place, though one suspects that a coup which dislodged Smith's government during or immediately after the Lancaster House Conference which led to the end of UDI and its replacement by a government committed to continuing the bush war (this time with the gloves off) would have led to a continuation of the war and, possibly, some sort of qualified (probably pyrrhic) victory for the Rhodesians.

These two examples demonstrate, in however broad a way, the importance of catching the tide of militancy on the flood. In the 1960s the British were far more concerned with fair play (and, one suspects, for the finer feelings of their white cousins in Rhodesia) than they appear to be now. They missed the chance to channel the wind of change blowing through the continent at this time, and the suffering which followed this *de facto* abdication of responsibility was immense and tragic. In 1970, faced with a distant but none the less important Arab country's imminent collapse under a revolutionary onslaught in the south, they had no such qualms and Sultan Said bin Taimur of Oman found himself ensconced in London's Dorchester Hotel pondering the irony of his hospitality at the hands of a country which had taken his Sultanate away and given it to his son, Qaboos.

MOBILIZATION

Slightly more tricky than the problem of setting a date is that of mobilizing one's forces without arousing suspicion. Every army in the world has some sort of Battle Preparation routine involving Orders groups, preparation of weapons and equipment, reconnaissance and deployment. A coup d'état is no different. The forces involved must be warned that H-Hour is approaching; they must be briefed properly; they must have time available in which to make their own plans and preparations; they must be able to fuel and arm their vehicles and AFV, to issue live ammunition to the infantry, ensure that radio batteries, water and medical supplies are all readily available, and to do the thousand and one other things vital to a smooth, well-run operation. All these preparations take time – the more so when they are being carried out in a clandestine fashion under the very noses (perhaps) of loyalist units.

One factor works in the plotters' favour; many of these procedures are tested regularly in field training or mobilization exercises. The only difference between these and live operations is the absence of live ammunition and, perhaps, wartime ration, water, fuel and supply scales. It is no coincidence that many coups d'état begin as apparently innocuous field exercises or other seemingly normal activities. Preparations for the Chilean coup, for example, were disguised as the prelude to an anti-terrorist sweep by air force ground troops and certain army units; other units were either remote enough geographically or isolated enough in their barracks for preparations to be carried out unnoticed.

It must be emphasized that in the majority of cases a full 'Preparation for Battle' routine is unnecessary – after all it isn't as if the plotters were to take on the entire Warsaw Pact. Even so, the 'P' rule beloved of British NCOs must be given due attention: 'Preparation and Planning Prevents Piss-Poor Performance'. The more complex the operation the more thorough must be the preparation, though even the simplest plan can founder on the rocks of one man's stupidity, as Mike Hoare found out in the Seychelles. Hoare's men carried their own weapons into the country, concealed in the bottoms of their sports bags. One might accuse Hoare of taking a dangerous risk in asking his men to do this, but for the purposes of this coup it remained the best – indeed the only – way of getting the weapons and ammunition into the country.

Hoare sent an advance party into the Seychelles up to a fortnight ahead of the main force; many of them carried their personal weapons, and on no less than four separate occasions a total of nine AK47 rifles had been smuggled successfully into the island, thus proving the validity of Hoare's plan. When the 45 men of the main force arrived there should have been no problem – and there wasn't, until one South African mercenary, who had never been abroad before and therefore did not realize the significance of the Green channel at Mahé Airport customs, went through the Red channel. He realized his mistake as soon as his bag was searched, but it was too late; the weapon was found. In his nervousness he compromised the other 44 men who were by now waiting for him in their tour party coaches outside the airport and the battle was on. Many people have criticized Hoare for his 'stupid' plan, but Hoare had proved that the plan could have worked; criticism should be levelled at his lack of foresight in not warning his men to go through the Green channel only.

Similarly, the French Generals in Algiers made a number of silly mistakes in the preparations for their *putsch* in 1961: an underground communications bunker in the grounds of one of the major government buildings was not discovered by the 1er REP until some hours after the coup began. An escaping loyalist government official managed to get into it and keep Prime Minister Debré in Paris up to date with developments in Algeria. It was not, one suspects, until General Challe (a former Commander-in-Chief in Algeria who must, therefore, have known about its existence) himself had taken control that the bunker was discovered. No one knows why he had not made this a priority target for the Assault Phase of his coup.

In other areas the Generals enjoyed the sort of luck any plotter can expect: the 1er REP's Commanding Officer was on leave so his second-in-command, a sympathizer with the *Algérie Française* cause, led the regiment instead. In Oran, however, the Army Commander was not a sympathizer and he was not on leave or absent from the country. His second-in-command was a sympathizer but was absent and so was not able either to subvert or neutralize his chief and bring the Oran garrison over to the plot.

The January 1966 coup attempt in Nigeria was quite professionally planned in many ways – the Chief of Police and Army Commander were sent on enforced leave so that they could not interfere with the plot – but the plotters failed to take the Chief of Staff, Major-General Johnny 'Ironside' Ironsi, into account. Although an Ibo like many of the other plotters, he was a highly professional and much-respected soldier and not one to become involved in unconstitutional activities. He had not been neutralized or subverted and, as a result, was able to react swiftly to news of the coup, covering the 13 miles from his officers' mess in Apapa, Lagos, to the infantry barracks at Ikeja near Lagos airport in record time, and effectively prevent the coup from achieving more than the murder of the Prime Minister, Sir Abubakar Tafawa Balewa. Sheer force of personality got Ironsi through the roadblocks set up by the plotters; not only was there an Intelligence failure in misreading Ironsi's character, but there seem to have been no orders given that he should be prevented from getting through. Somebody slipped up at the Orders Group and the coup failed as a result. Interestingly enough, however, although the coup was a failure it ended up with Ironsi running the country at the request of the acting president (President Azikiwe was absent in London convalescing after an operation).

During their *Tancazo* of June 1973, the Chilean 2nd Armoured Regiment went into action in a terrible state. Some vehicles had not been fuelled and at least one tank stopped at a roadside filling-station on its way to the Moneda Palace in Santiago to extract petrol from the hapless attendant at cannon-point. Conversely, the successful plotters who overthrew Allende three months later left very little to chance; squads of soldiers visited radio stations operated by the Socialist and Communist parties under the pretext of searching for illegal arms. They arrived just after the stations went off the air for the night, stayed for only an hour or so and left apologetically, with empty hands. The following morning, however, when Allende was trying to rally support in the face of the armed forces' coup, the stations were found to have been sabotaged.

These examples show us the importance of preparation as well as planning and with them in mind let us pass on to the next stage of the plot – its execution.

8
EXECUTION
Mission – The Assault

The British Army has a format for Operational Orders which covers just about everything the soldier receiving them needs to know about what he is to do next. At first glance the orders sequence seems a little strange for our purposes – the cart is put before the horse in a way that wouldn't occur in a narrative account of a real coup d'état – but let us stick with it because, from from your own, purely operational, point of view, it meets our needs admirably. The sequence runs like this:

- **Ground**
- **Situation**
  - *Enemy forces*
  - *Friendly forces*
- **Mission**
- **Execution**
  - *Outline*
  - *Detail*
- **Logistics**
- **Command and Signals**
- **Co-ordinating Instructions**

We are not concerned here with the giving of orders – not exclusively, at any rate – but with their execution. Bearing in mind that the Co-ordinating Instructions, Command and Signals annexes and Logistics orders must normally be acted upon before the Missions can be carried out, let us go through the 'O' sequence.

GROUND

The ground you will be fighting on is likely to be urban in nature; buildings will be large, closely spaced and, quite possibly, contain a high density of civilians. Between the buildings will be narrow stretches of tarmac suitable for wheeled vehicles; there may also be larger areas of open ground – parks and gardens – containing trees, bushes and small stretches of water. The potential battlefield will be, in some ways, multi-dimensional; most buildings will have a number of storeys and windows from which concealed troops will be able to bring effective fire to bear upon an enemy at street level. Buildings aid concealment of ambushers and fugitives and are time-consuming to search and clear. Depending upon the amount of firepower available to the plotters, buildings may also be easy to protect and defend.

Below ground there may be an urban transport system such as the Paris Métro or London Underground. The various stations and depots may be useful escape routes or lying-up points for an enemy.

Within the buildings the environment will be not dissimilar to that encountered on the streets: small, enclosed areas connected by doors set in opaque walls into which are set the occasional window which allows one not only to observe an enemy and perhaps shoot at him but also to be shot by him.

In a sense, fighting in the city will be not unlike fighting in the jungle, except that the jungle has no staircases.

Any actual fighting in the city must, therefore, be discouraged for the following reasons: it will be time-consuming, costly in ammunition and lives, liable to antagonize the population to an unacceptable degree and require more fighting men than most plotters can spare. Besides this, urban warfare (what the British Army calls Fighting in Built-up Areas, or FIBUA) demands specific training of a highly professional order; there is no guarantee that any of the troops under the plotters' command will have enjoyed this training so a full-blooded FIBUA-style engagement is liable to delay the progress of the coup unacceptably and to cause comparatively high numbers of casualties. The only circumstances under which the prospect of a FIBUA-type engagement may be slightly attractive are where the tactical initiative lies with the plotters; that is, where there has been time to prepare adequate defences against an enemy whom one knows for sure is not expecting resistance when he enters the city. Even then, the potential must exist for a strong counter-attack which will bring the enemy to the bargaining table before such an engagement is considered to be a desirable option.

What does this tell us about the type of operation you will be carrying out? First of all that, once troops are committed to the coup attempt, they must not, if possible, be drawn into street battles. Proper Intelligence and good planning will ensure, one trusts, that the coup will be swift and bloodless. If it is not, if there remain isolated pockets of armed resistance, these may be ignored for a short time so long as they are not a danger to the coup itself. Once the new government is in power and has begun to establish its authority over the population, these pockets can be either persuaded to surrender or attacked by a concentration of force which was probably unavailable to the plotters during the Assault and Continuation Phases.

More serious levels of resistance, especially by large units of the loyalist forces, demand an instant reaction from the plotters so that the coup can proceed as quickly as possible. If a pocket of resistance outnumbers the plotters' forces, something has gone seriously wrong; either a loyalist unit has appeared on the scene unexpectedly (bad luck or poor Intelligence), or a unit which was gauged originally to be either sympathetic to the coup or apathetic enough to be thought neutral has changed colour. This is an Intelligence failure also. A head-on confrontation should be avoided, if possible, and delaying tactics used to buy time while as many Priority A targets as possible are taken. With these in the plotters' hands it may be possible then to treat with the loyalists or simply present them with a *fait accompli*; this may encourage them to give up the idea of fighting and return to barracks.

Unless there are known to be loyalist units in or near a major target which will fight the plotters as hard as they can (as was the case with

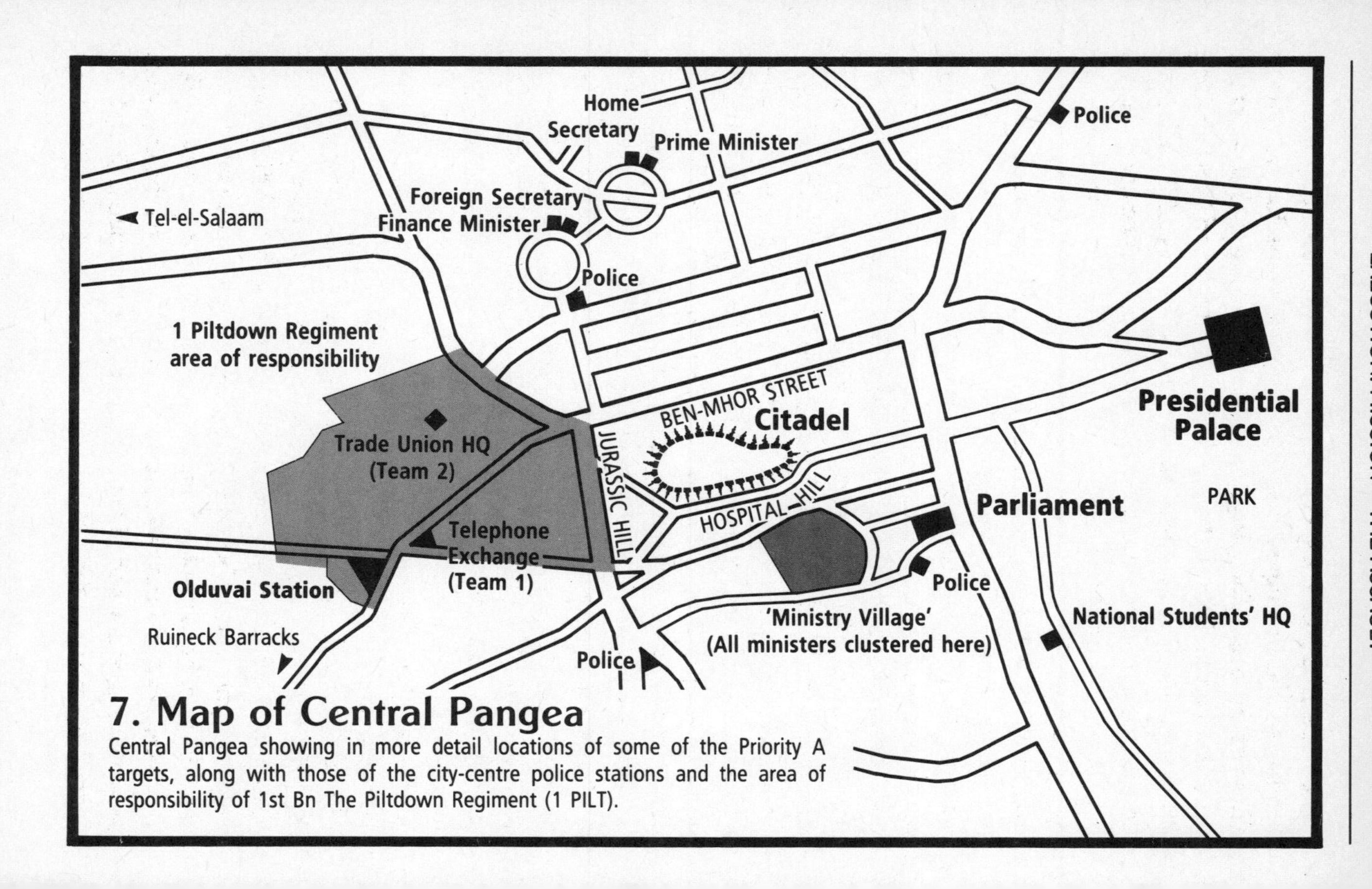

7. Map of Central Pangea

Central Pangea showing in more detail locations of some of the Priority A targets, along with those of the city-centre police stations and the area of responsibility of 1st Bn The Piltdown Regiment (1 PILT).

the Carabineros protecting President Allende of Chile in 1973), street-fighting should not figure prominently in the plans for the Assault Phase of the coup. The plan should, however, take into account the possible need to defend, during the Continuation and Consolidation Phases, positions which were taken during the Assault Phase. This depends very much on the quality of one's Intelligence appreciation, however, and the notional ORBAT of Friendly and Enemy forces you have drawn up.

One aspect of 'Ground' which must not be ignored is that of physical geography. The map of Pangea on page 62 shows the rough location of particular features and notional targets. The map reproduced here shows in more detail their location and approaches. It will be seen that there are certain nodal points in the road system (Pangea has no Métro) by which, if the plotters have proper control over them, they can control the entire sector in question. Once a certain area has been cleared or 'sanitized', it is not necessary to post a tank on every street corner; a few men, yes, to ensure that residents of the area do not try to resist, but not armour. Tanks, AFVs, overt displays of real military muscle can be confined to those areas visible from the known and likely approach routes of loyalist forces.

Where possible, such points should be chosen not just for their psychological effect on civilians and loyalist troops and for their domination of particular roads and avenues, but should offer some tactical advantage: thus a defensive position set up at the bottom of Jurassic Hill, for example, should be backed up by either AFV or anti-armour weapons sited to bring enfilade fire on an enemy approaching from the west and north-west.

All this assumes, of course, the worst case: a coup carried out in the full knowledge that loyalist forces close to the main centres of operations have not been neutralized or subverted and that a swift, violent response must be expected. This will not usually be the case and it is probably a waste of time and effort to divert precious troops to the seizing and fortification of strong points around the city when the likelihood of any sort of armed response to the coup is likely to be negligible for a number of hours. A case in point would be the situation where the Tectonic Knights, the Ruineck garrison and the Tel-el-Salaam headquarters have all been penetrated and either neutralized or subverted. By the time more distant units have heard about the coup it will be over and they will be confronted with a *fait accompli.* If they refuse to accept this, a number of troops from all three bases can be deployed to resist them once Priority A and B targets are secure. Such deployments would, of course, become Priority C objectives.

In the case of the Tel-el-Salaam garrison and elements of the Ruineck garrison, men, artillery and armour could, if absolutely necessary, be deployed as an initial screen and, later, a covering force against loyalist reaction as part of their Priority A tasks. The requirement to do so should be examined as part of the overall Intelligence appreciation. The appreciation must take into account some of the major characteristics of units or formations liable to intervene: their location, the means of transport available to them, their likely avenues of approach, their likely response time and, thus, the best positions from which to engage them. A tactically difficult position close to the centre of the action is sometimes preferable, when the plotters' lines of communication are tenuous, to an ideal but insupportable position farther away but outside the reach of the plotters' logistical machine.

It will be seen from this passage that a sound appreciation of the nature of the ground on which you will be operating is vital. The only thing more important than a close recce of the ground is an understanding of the problems and prospects it poses to a loyalist force moving to counter the coup. For example, it may be necessary only to defend or destroy a couple of critical bridges over rivers encircling the defended area, thereby imposing further delay upon the loyalists by their need to mount an assault river crossing. Any attempt to do so will leave them vulnerable and may incease the likelihood of the civil war which both sides should be trying to prevent.

In short, the ground should be used to present a series of obstacles to the loyalists, the surmounting of which presents a tactical problem leading to a warlike deployment of their field assets. They must be made aware that every time they are forced to do so they are lowering the threshold of violence and are coming closer to the use of force (and hence the prospect of civil war) to wrest back the tactical initiative. The harder they have to work to get through a series of well-sited natural and man-made barriers, the more they must be made to feel that it simply isn't worth it.

SITUATION – ENEMY FORCES

By 'Enemy Forces' we mean those units which will not sit on the fence awaiting the outcome of your venture before showing their hand; who will make every attempt to take immediate and direct action against you. For one reason or another (it may be a constitutional reason, or simply loyalty to the head of state you are trying to overthrow) they do not like this coup happening and will try to stop it. Constitutionalists, unless they are extremely patriotic, will, as often as not, make terms in order to preserve the unity of the country and the armed forces, if they can be persuaded that they have no chance of success and that the coup is a good thing.

The 'President's Own', however, are liable to feel a greater institutional and personal loyalty to the head of state and may therefore display greater tenacity in the battle to support or restore him, especially if he remains at large after the Assault Phase and is in a position to rally support and whip up his or her forces into a fanatical frenzy. Such adversaries are dangerous. They can allow themselves to be martyred and use the publicity to create a groundswell of opinion in the head of state's – or the cause's – favour, which may be used against the plotters, either immediately or, to perhaps greater effect, in the future. When carrying out an appreciation of the enemy forces' numbers, strength and capability, the capacity for fanaticism of this kind (typified by the reaction of the International Left to Allende's overthrow in Chile) must be borne in mind. One partial answer to this problem is to make sure that the head of state is well and truly neutralized at the outset, either through abduction as a Priority A target or through his absence from the country. It helps also to make clear in good faith that the head of state's supporters will not suffer for their loyalty to him.

At a more mundane level you need to know what the loyalists can deploy against you and what you need to do about it. Are the loyalists a tank regiment? If so, you will need tanks of your own or anti-tank weapons. Are they an infantry regiment? If so you will need to prepare for a battle in the streets and cellars of the city, using steady troops who will not baulk at the use of submachine-gun, pistol, bayonet and grenade. Are the loyalists composed mainly of the air force? In that case, you might be in trouble, unless your own troops have control over some of the anti-aircraft weapons or unless you can neutralize the airfields. The Navy? Can their big guns or strike aircraft reach you at an inland or coastal capital? Then you may need to deploy heavy artillery against the ships or naval air bases. Are troop-carrying helicopters available to the loyalists in sufficient numbers and with sufficient fuel and logistics support to mount an airborne assault? If so, you must bear in mind the theory and doctrines concerning airborne forces and their deployment, and take the appropriate tactical measures (mining potential landing zones, covering them with machine-gun or artillery fire, etc.).

The problems with 'Enemy Forces' are manifold and no solution can be proposed until you know who they are, where they are, what they are capable of doing and whether or not they are likely to do it. The key lies in carrying out your Intelligence appreciation properly.

SITUATION – FRIENDLY FORCES

You know who your friends are – don't you? Don't be too sure! Yes, you have an order of battle of the troops whom you know are committed your cause, but what about the others, the fence-sitters? To become your friends they need only do nothing. Can you guarantee that they will do so? Especially if the enemy comes across them and makes all sorts of threats towards their commanders? I think not. Let us procrastinate for a moment and look at the people you know are 'Friendly Forces'.

These will be units whose officers and men have made a formal commitment to the plot and whose presence in your own ORBAT is a vital part of your plan for the coup. Typically, they will be a diverse lot: some infantry from here, armour from there, a few engineers, gunners, donkey-wallopers and so on – not a homogeneous body of men at all, in all probability. What can you achieve with them? The answer depends very much on two things – circumstances, to which any enterprise is a hostage in some way, and the quality and perception of the operational leadership. It must not be forgotten that, for men acting under pressure and in conditions of fear and stress (which is a typical frame of mind for anybody engaged in a treasonable activity), unit solidarity and a reassuring adherence to a known and trusted routine are vitally important. One does not, therefore, ask an ordnance field park stores clerk to carry out a commando's job and nor does one ask a troop of tankers, fighting in the infantry role, to put a city-centre building into a state of defence against an infantry assault. Nor does one mix and match the various arms under temporary and untried commanders in an *ad hoc* command structure if one can possibly help it. Remember that in the British Army even highlanders, paratroopers and Gurkhas have all been known to perform poorly in the past when faced with poor leadership and incompetent man-management. One suits the horse to the course, naturally. Let us assume that, to 'take out' Pangea the plotters have at their disposal the following forces:

3 Battalions of infantry.
1 Field ambulance.
1 Regiment of M-48 tanks.
1 Field company of military police.
1 Regiment of scout cars (the Tectonic Knights).
1 Field squadron of engineers.
1 Heavy plant troop of engineers.
1 Regiment of light artillery.
1 Signal squadron.
1 Ordnance field park.
1 Transport squadron.

Added to this they can count upon the facilities of one military hospital, one academy of higher military studies, and (most importantly) a brigade headquarters and a local district headquarters (divorced, of course, from army headquarters at Tel-el-Salaam).

They have at their disposal, then, a reinforced brigade group. If the brigade commander is part of the plot and in charge of his own men, the 'O' Group should pass easily and confidently, and the entire formation will tend to act with something approaching one mind. The commander can make his own orders knowing that liaison, command and control will be quite harmonious.

Let us suppose, however, that the figures above, while amounting to a conventional reinforced brigade group, consist not of three battalions of infantry but nine or twelve companies of infantry from some half-a-dozen different units and that the supporting arms are merely accretions of individuals and small sections approximating to about the nominal strength on the ORBAT shown above. What then? The men will obey orders, of course, but will they work effectively together? Will they trust one another? Will command and control be as efficient as with a fully integrated set of sub-units in a brigade? Probably not. The problem facing the operational commander in this coup is to make the troops work together, to get them to achieve their objectives, but without over-taxing their morale, *esprit de corps* and cohesion.

This is where the junior NCOs and officers come into their own. They will be required to maintain the cohesion of their own little sub-units while getting on with the job in hand. The accepted method of getting the best out of people in such a situation is to play on their need of fellowship, in other words to lump all the engineers together under the senior sapper, the infantry according to parent regiments, and so on; then to maintain the small sub-units as far as possible, and with their usual commanders whether these be lance-corporals or majors. If Lance-Corporal Snooks has come over to the plot with a section from an engineer recce troop, the troop should be given an engineer task consistent with its size, training and original role, and Snooks should receive his orders from a sapper officer or senior NCO who can liaise with the senior plotters in provision of whatever logistics assets are required.

One does not place a troop of gunners, who have locked their own officers up, under the command of a junior subaltern from a signals squadron. If necessary, give the senior NCO or warrant officer present the temporary status of local artillery commander (if he is capable of fighting his troop of guns properly), and build him into the command structure. Not only will he have more confidence in the coup's leadership, but he will transmit this confidence to his men, and the firepower he commands will be a still greater asset to the plot. Finally, under no circumstances should two élite and mutually antagonistic regiments be mixed unless there is absolute confidence that they will work closely and harmoniously together. If elements of, say, the paratroops are to be integrated with elements of the mountain corps, the coup's leaders must make absolutely certain the officer in charge is sympathetic to the *amour propre* of both and does not antagonize one or other regiment unncessarily. One thinks here of the Algiers coup of 1961 in which the antagonism between the Foreign Legion and the paratroops and the mass of conscripts and ordinary line regiments was such that cohesion was almost impossible to achieve and totally impossible to maintain. General Challe confidently expected to have 40,000 men under his command – he ended up with about 12,000, all from the Réserve Générale (Paras and Legion, mainly), a figure which dwindled steadily over the five days he was running Algiers.

There is a great deal of sense in insisting that all troops wear a visible marker such as an armband or a badge on their helmets, which not only distinguishes them from the enemy but gives them a feeling of togetherness, or *esprit de corps*. The sticking of roses down the muzzles of rifle barrels is not to be encouraged, however!

MISSION

The most important part of any military operation is selection and maintenance of aim. The troops must be told what the object of the operation is, not just what their own little part in it will be. Unanimity of intention is vital in a venture such as a coup d'état. Every soldier must be made aware that his job is not just to secure the TV studios, for example, but to help overthrow the government. Thus, when the studios are secure they cannot rest on their laurels – they must get on with a secondary task which will assist materially the cause of the plot.

It must be made clear to the men that there is no room in the initial stages of the plot for pettiness, settling of old scores and internecine rivalries between various plotters or between plotters and the loyalists. It must be impressed upon the men that unless the Priority A targets are taken successfully, and unless the Assault Phase is a total or substantial success, the rest of the plot may come to nothing. Skimping on a Priority A target simply so that the men can then get on with looting at their Priority B target is not on: threats of dire punishment for dereliction of duty must, if necessary, be uttered and subsequently carried out. One can't make an omelette, so we are told, without breaking eggs, and in a venture such as a coup d'état a little summary justice administered to offenders *pour encourager les autres* may go a long way. Apart from anything else it may also frighten the population and any loyalists who witness it, and create a useful impression of ruthlessness and professionalism.

If one goes about administering field punishment to co-conspirators, however, it may turn the victim's colleagues against you. It might even convince the loyalists that no quarter is to be given or taken and so encourage desperate resistance. The key to this little conundrum lies in avoiding it in the first place – by making sure that the plan is right, that the Intelligence is right, that the briefing is right and that the leadership is right.

The missions given to separate parts of the plotters' forces will, of course, differ substantially. The overall mission is 'To overthrow the government and replace it with a new one.' As its part in achieving the overall mission, the 1st Battalion the Piltdown Regiment (1 PILT) might be ordered to 'Secure the Western part of Central Pangea, including Olduvai railway station and the Ministry of Administrative

Affairs'. A Company 1 PILT may then be tasked with taking out the station; B Company with taking out the ministry, and C Company with the two police stations in the area. The secondary (Priority B) objectives would then be taken by detachments from appropriate sub-units while the remainder of the battalion sets about putting the area in a state of defence or taking out Priority C targets. The mortar platoon of Support Company could be detached to provide manpower and, subsequently, fire support for the Cro-Magnon Cavalry Regiment, whose tanks and supporting infantry company are sealing off the main road from the west. And so on.

If an unexpected pocket of resistance is discovered in Central Pangea which needs dealing with urgently, it may be necessary to tell the CO of 1 PILT to ignore his orders completely and send one of his companies back into the city to deal with it so that his rear is secure and the other units involved can get on with what may be more critical jobs. Flexibility is vitally important and the importance of good communications and correct reporting procedures is paramount; the overall commander must have a clear tactical picture at all times if he is to direct the coup successfully. In order to achieve this during the Assault Phase it may be necessary to adopt highly unorthodox reporting procedures and command structures, a problem covered under 'Signals'.

It is normal to divide an area of operations between several sub-units, their commanders becoming the local area commanders as a result. If this system is adopted for the purposes of the coup, every mission, every target, within the operational area becomes the responsibility of the local commander. In the case of 1 PILT this may pose few problems, but in say, the centre of Pangea, where the highest proportion of Priority A targets is grouped, there might be a little too much responsibility for one man or one unit. Is there a case for briefing one set of units to take out all Priority A targets, wherever they may be in the city, without reference to local area commanders (whose responsibility would then be to the Priority B and C targets)? Perhaps, but having two independent groups of fighting men operating in the same area with different orders and different targets, especially when time to prepare the operation has necessarily been limited and certain co-ordinating details may not have been worked out properly, is dangerous.

On reflection, unless particular circumstances dictate otherwise, it is best to allocate targets on a geographical basis to local area commanders and then allocate to these figures the assets necessary to take them out. If a re-allocation of resources becomes necessary later on, this can be arranged by the overall commander.

EXECUTION – OUTLINE

Let us imagine ourselves for a moment in the shoes of Mike Hoare during his main briefing for the Seychelles coup of 1981. With his men assembled in Johannesburg he held his briefing the night before the main force flew out to the island. The briefing might have gone something like this.

- **Ground:** which everybody would then have a chance to inspect during their week or so on the island and which would thus have held very few surprises, except for the layout of particular buildings and point targets.
- **Situation – Enemy Forces:** which most of the men would be familiar with, having had a chance to look around and observe the Tanzanian and Seychellois troops in situ.
- **Situation – Friendly Forces:** the only unknown aspect would have been the level of material support they could expect from the local resistance movement.
- **Mission:** 'To seize complete control of the island of Mahé', which most of them already knew.
- **Execution – Outline:** for which details were, understandably, scarce until the briefing. 'Simultaneous assaults upon the airport and main army barracks, the radio station, the army headquarters and Victoria Barracks and State House, followed by simultaneous assaults on the Presidential Palace and the Cable and Wireless Office where we shall establish our Headquarters.'

This particular part of the briefing is vitally important, whatever the operation is going to be. Everybody now knows the Mission. They know roughly how it is going to be carried out and the reasons for the planning decisions (from Enemy Forces, Friendly Forces and Ground). They know what the main targets are so the general thrust of the operation can be impressed upon them as well as the need to support friendly units who run into problems while carrying out critical tasks, and what those critical tasks are likely to be. The men know where they fit in to the bigger picture and where, if there is a sudden problem or a complete breakdown in communications, their individual initiative is best directed.

EXECUTION – DETAIL

In the context of Mike Hoare's plan, the detailed outline of his plan has been given elsewhere. The main force was to be divided into two teams: one to take out the airport and main barracks; the other to take out State House, Victoria Barracks and Cable and Wireless. A third group, the Advance Party in fact, would take out the radio station. Thus, everybody now knew where everybody else was supposed to be, what they were supposed to be doing, what the main priorities were for their own group and what to watch out for if any of the other groups failed in any of their tasks.

Also, each group had a local responsibility which encompassed Priority A, B and C targets. Group II, for example, eighteen men strong, would be subdivided into three sections: 1 Section, consisting of 12 men, was tasked with taking out first the army barracks (where a substantial armoury and logistics base was located) and then the airport perimeter; 2 Section, consisting of just four men, would take out the two houses inside the barracks where the Tanzanian soldiers were actually billeted. While 1 Section was carrying out its tasks, a two-man air control team would storm the control tower (if 'storm' is not too strong a word for an assault on an undefended facility) and assume immediate control of all air movements while waiting for the airport perimeter to be secured. So we have our Priority A target identified (the army barracks and the billets inside them); our Priority B target (the airport perimeter); and our Priority C target (the airport control tower).

Group III, which was tasked with securing State House, army headquarters and Victoria Barracks, consisted of some 26 men. The most important, Priority A, target was State House. At the cabinet meeting in progress there at the time would be not only the Minister of Defence, Ogilvy Berlouis, but also the Army Chief of Staff and the Minister of Education and Information, James Michel. Take them out and the ability of army HQ to react to the coup would be severely depleted; take out also both the HQ and the nearby barracks, and simultaneously destroy communications between them and the 16 troops guarding the radio station, and the decoupling of the entire Seychelles Army would be complete.

The other Priority B targets for Group III would have been the presidential palace, where President René's family and personal entourage were located, and the Cable and Wireless office which was undefended.

Significantly, Group I – the Advance Party – had only one target, possibly the most important of all: the radio station and its 16 guards. The Advance Party had made a comprehensive reconnaissance of this target, and included in their number a broadcasting engineer who, once the station was secure, would broadcast the tape made by Jimmy Mancham assuring the Seychellois that he was on the island and that René was, figuratively speaking at least, on the way out. The psychological effect of such an announcement on the Seychellois was calculated shrewdly; most – including the police, who had a profound contempt for the Seychelles Army – disliked René and would have made themselves available if required to assist the mercenaries and the *Mouvement pour la Résistance*.

Presented with a *fait accompli*, faced with a hostile population, totally confused as to what was going on and who and where the enemy were, the last pockets of resistance would either have given up or dwindled to the stage where they could be defeated easily by Hoare's men.

In just about every way, then, the operational planning of Hoare's coup was that of the classical coup d'état. The Priority A targets would have been taken almost simultaneously and within minutes of H-Hour, thus largely paralyzing any immediate and effective resistance, and careful use of the radio would have initiated a snowballing of support for the coup – the operation would, in effect, have become a self-sustaining mechanism.

Contrast this with Denard's Benin coup attempt (which at least took place, in fairness to Denard!) His plan, although excellent on paper, was not flexible enough to take into account the Intelligence failure which President Kerekou's absence from the presidential palace represented, and apparently included no provision to take the radio station during the Assault Phase. For some unknown reason the radio station, 'Voice of the Revolution', was relegated to Priority B status (or lower); this, despite the fact that the psychological effect of an immediate broadcast to the population could have a huge destabilizing effect on resistance while the battle was in progress, was well known to Denard. The incoming President, M. Gratien Pognon, flew in with the mercenaries, his prepared speech in his briefcase, and waited at the airport for Kerekou's death and the capture of the radio station. Had he been taken straight to the radio station (something like half the mercenary force stayed at Cotonou airport doing nothing except guard it), it is quite possible that Kerekou would have fallen and that President Eyadema of Togo would have sent his own troops into Benin to help stabilize the situation and see President Pognon installed safely.

Bob Denard's failure in Benin is an excellent example of how not to plan a coup and contains many lessons. What makes this failure all the more remarkable (or, perhaps, makes some of his earlier successes all the more remarkable, if he planned them the same way) is the fact that he was a devotee of Frederick Forsyth, had read *The Dogs of War* and in fact had used some of the fictional names and terms invented by Forsyth himself in the novel to disguise his own intentions when drawing up the original plan for this coup. Forsyth got it right, in outline; Denard, inexplicably, got it wrong.

Chile is an interesting case study in this same context. The Chilean armed forces succeeded in silencing most of the pro-Allende radio stations during the night preceding the coup, and carried out many of the preparations for the coup with textbook efficiency. Interestingly, however, they did not use the radio only to appeal directly to the people for support (they had no need of physical support, in any case), but also used their broadcasts to give Allende the chance to surrender. They gave Allende a way out, if he wanted it. He didn't. Allende was ensconced in the Moneda Palace, was fully aware of what was going on, but counted on the support of 'the People' (his own people, at any rate). It wasn't forthcoming, and what began as a clash of wills – the armed forces *v.* Allende – became a fire fight in which Allende was able to command the sympathy of almost the entire world by representing himself as an elected president, in his own presidential palace, being attacked by a crew of unconstitutional, power-hungry soldiers.

Why, one asks, did the armed forces not send a squad of special forces into Allende's residence at Tomas Moro and lock him up, or put him on a plane bound for Cuba? They could have taken over the country bloodlessly, smoothly and without the huge media coverage which so inflamed both Chilean Communists and liberal world opinion. In an otherwise well-run coup this one mistake made a huge amount of difference to the perception of the Chilean armed forces in the world's eyes, and the level of political violence inspired by the so-called resistance movements in Chile thereafter. If, as has been suggested privately to the author, the Generals and Admirals were trying merely to be chivalrous in their dealings with Allende, they over-estimated the man; there is little chivalry in politics – of whatever complexion – and they failed to realize the value to a cause of somebody's martyrdom.

What, then, have we learned about this particular part of the Execution of a coup d'état? Significantly, we have spent more time in discussion of military psychology and detailed planning than in actual execution. Does this suggest then, given the right plan and good leaders, that the actual execution is a walk-over? By no means.

But one must bear in mind the fact that the majority of coup targets will be comparatively undefended and so any sort of resistance is liable to be low once the Assault Phase is over and before more distant loyalists can get their collective act together.

If there is a lesson to be learned from this Chapter it must be this: the right plan, even when executed in a somewhat slipshod or unprofessional manner, can remove the need to do battle (initially, at least), and the presentation of a *fait accompli* may obviate the need for any fighting at all.

LOGISTICS

Our next major heading in the 'O' Sequence is always an unglamorous subject, but one which the plotter ignores at his peril. Almost every major coup d'état involving a complete or nearly complete military unit has enjoyed access to the unit's vehicles, fuel, ammunition and other combat supplies. If one takes the British Army as an example, it will be found that each company group in a battalion has its own vehicles and an armoury for its weapons. The battalion's signals platoon will have stocks of radios and batteries while the Intelligence cell will have its own methods of gathering and disseminating information and maps. The motor transport platoon will have all the heavy vehicles, while the assault pioneers will have their own limited engineer stores. Put all these assets together and one has a formidable capability to deploy and fight. In an infantry brigade there will be an ordnance field park, a transport squadron and supporting arms fielding heavy weapons, all of which enhance enormously the fighting power and mobility available to the individual battalions.

This capability is useless, however, without two things: fuel and ammunition. There may be a fuel point within the brigade or battalion area, but this is often not the case. In an area like London, for example, dispersed sub-units of the Territorial Army rely frequently on fuel stocks held at a small number of local depots and major barracks complexes, and the same applies to regular units.

Where ammunition is concerned, British soldiers have very little access to it without proper authority. Small arms ammunition, artillery and AFV ammunition and mortar ammunition – blank and ball – tends to be kept under secure guard in central depots spread around the country. Only units with a specific requirement for rapid access to live ammunition keep theirs to hand – SAS counter-revolutionary warfare (CRW) teams, quick-reaction force teams near docks or airports, and so on. Paradoxically, for a country whose policemen are traditionally unarmed, certain police units (notably the Diplomatic Protection Group, tasked with protecting VIPs and the Royal Family, and elements of the Flying Squad and Special Branch) may have better and quicker access to firearms and ammunition than the majority of soldiers.

While Britain represents one extreme example of a plotter's logistical problems, it cannot be assumed that other armies may not be similarly hamstrung. A small army dispersed over a wide area will naturally have ammunition and logistics depots located at or near major troop concentrations, especially in countries where communications and transport between locations is difficult. If one takes the British example again, the garrison in Belize probably represents something closer to the opposite extreme, which is common in other parts of the world: infantry, artillery and light armour sub-units dispersed widely in a country whose terrain is difficult and through which vehicle movement is all but impossible at certain times of the year. In the event of an incursion by Guatemalan forces (government or rebels!) each sub-unit must be able to take independent action to hold the line while support is called up. It is not inconceivable that a company commander who goes mad in one of the up-country locations could try to send a column into Belize City to overthrow the government – he would certainly have no trouble getting access to live ammunition.

Most countries that have experienced coups d'état lie between these two extremes, which means in turn that in many cases troops had to get hold of ammunition by subterfuge. The beauty of having a senior officer on the scene as part of the plot is that he can give the necessary orders to the depot concerned to release the ammunition to his troops. Ammunition, like fuel, can be issued over a period of days to various elements of the main force so long as adequate warning is given: vehicles can be filled up in an irregular sequence then left alone until the big day without anybody being any the wiser; ammunition can be issued to troops under the cover of a live firing exercise taking place in the very near future. If necessary, the men can simply roll up at the ammunition depot the night before the coup, brandishing their orders from a senior officer and demanding what they want.

Ammunition is, of course, a sensitive commodity which is strictly controlled and issued mainly for use under carefully defined conditions. The plotters must know something about the way ammunition is stored and administered before they even consider the logistics phase of their plan. They must have some strategy for getting hold of the right ammunition in the right quantities without anybody realizing what they are up to.

COMMAND AND SIGNALS

This is one of the most important aspects of the coup d'état once it is under way. The officers and men carrying out the coup must know, first of all, which other units are involved, or at the very least how to recognize them, and they must know who their commanders are. They must also be familiar with the terrain – which, in this context, means having access to reasonably good maps – and they must know who their immediate superiors and subordinates are for the purpose of passing messages and orders. Finally the signals system must be worked out minutely so that everybody who needs to can talk to somebody else.

All this might seem a little obvious, but frightened men (and you cannot assume that your troops are not frightened at what they are doing) working in the darkened streets of a city they don't know are prone to do silly things, like shooting at friendly forces. More

8. The Pangea Coup: Communications Network

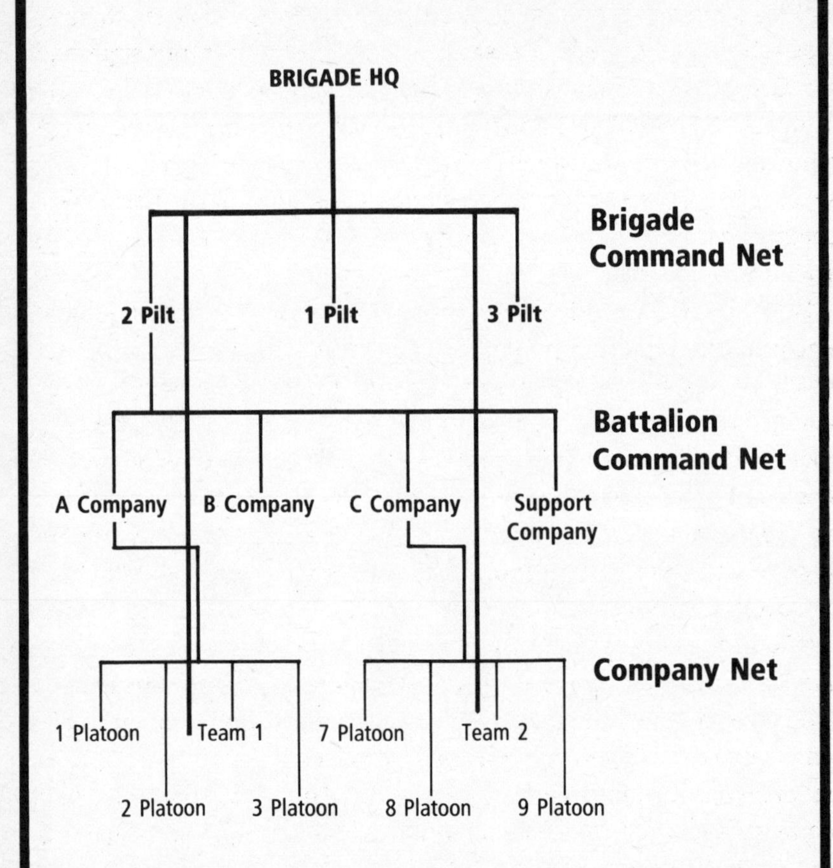

The Pangea Coup: communications network of 1 PILT. Note how Teams 1 and 2 report directly to Brigade HQ using the Brigade command net, thus ensuring that HQ 1 PILT is kept up to date simultaneously on developments in their areas without depriving the Brigade Commander of accurate, timely information on the progress of critical parts of the Assault Phase of the coup.

importantly, they must be able to report to their superiors accurately and quickly any developments in their particular area.

It has been suggested that local area commanders should carry the responsibility for all operations in their own district; this would mean that the supreme commander receives information only from three or four subordinates. Such a system is excellent in both principle and practice, but there may be times when he needs to know on a minute by minute basis what is happening around certain Priority A targets. A reporting system in which a section commander's message of success in taking out the head of state goes up through four or five command levels is hardly secure, especially where loyalists may be listening in covertly.

Better by far, for at least part of the operation, is an arrangement where teams under the command of the local area commander, but which are tasked with taking out specific Priority A targets, use the same command net as their superiors reporting back to the supreme commander. In this way urgent radio traffic is confined to only a single radio net, while the area commanders are kept simultaneously up to date with what is happening on 'their patch'. A typical reporting system is shown on page 158. What the system highlights is the use of covert teams operating in advance of the main force. It is a constant mystery to many people why some coups d'état are so unnecessarily messy; a swift, surgical strike by a small team of men can 'take out' the head of state and certain point targets with remarkable ease, given the right circumstances, and that their use has not been more widespread is inexplicable. The Chileans used covert teams to sabotage radio stations and certain telephone exchanges (though not those in Santiago), but not to take out Allende himself and his senior lieutenants. Mike Hoare had no need of them. The Nigerians seem not to have used them and nor did the French Generals in Algiers.

One thing the Generals did make use of in Algiers was the local knowledge of the *France Résistance* activists. Many of the Legionnaires from 1er REP who took part in the coup were not familiar with the government quarter of the city and so FR guides met the troops at rendezvous throughout the city and led them, two guides to a target, to the objectives.

Regarding the supreme commander and his own command and control problems, one would probably feel justified in stating that an orthodox headquarters structure with a secure base is not only an ideal but a necessity. A complex plan with reports coming in from and orders going out to numerous sub-units demands slick organization at the top so that reports can be collated and presented to the commander in the most quickly assimilated form and so that he can react to developments with commensurate speed. Mike Hoare planned to use the Cable and Wireless offices in Victoria as his headquarters, but this had to be taken first. General Pinochet used the Army Telecommunications School in Penalolen, just outside Santiago, as his headquarters, while the Air Force Commander, General Leigh, set up his HQ in the Headquarters of Number 10 Air Group at the Academy of Air Warfare in the Santiago suburb of Las Condes. Communications between the two and between them and the Naval HQ at Valparaiso was maintained by a team working at the Ministry of Defence which was in the plotter's hands from the very start.

The command and control exercised during the Chilean coup seems to have been exemplary and this is obviously a model which other plotters might follow, if they are given the chance. The vital elements were all there; secure radio and landline communications between all units and their commanders, and excellent liaison between the three services. Reporting was fast and accurate and there were plenty of staff available to do the mundane jobs like maintaining logs and marking up maps while the commanders exercised their minds and their authority.

CO-ORDINATING INSTRUCTIONS

Even the best-laid plans end up with people tripping over one another's or their own feet. In effect, the co-ordinating instructions are a way of telling people that they will not be sent off to do a job and then forgotten about until somebody has time to give them more thought. It is important for the subordinate commanders to know where other friendly units are, when they will be there, where and when the spare rations and ammunition will be and in what condition, and when other sub-units will be crossing their patch and which direction they should be coming from. This is all basic stuff and needs no elaboration here; it is covered by the one word, Liaison, which is most frequently ignored, abused or paid lip-service to by unprofessional soldiery.

Liaison has to be close enough to prevent friendly forces shooting at one another ('blue on blue contacts'), or two units ignoring a vital target, each believing the other is tackling it.

ORDERS

The 'O' Group will probably be one of the most important parts of the entire operation. However good or bad a plan is, its execution may depend very much on the quality of the orders the men receive. An orders sequence like the outline above covers all the main points of the plan and each unit or sub-unit's part in it, but the way in which they are given makes a huge difference to their reception and execution. Every soldier knows officers from whom he has received formal orders, and can probably classify these officers according to the alacrity with which he will obey the orders, no matter how distasteful. Field Marshal Mongomery must have been one of the best commanders in this respect. He could inspire men, command their devotion and affection and thus generate a greater concentration on the task in hand than almost any of his contemporaries.

Although subject to many of the weaknesses to which humankind is prey (hubris being not the least among them), Monty knew how to get an army on to its feet and running, and the man selected to command the coup must be somebody of a similar stature. Much will depend upon the example set by subordinate commanders, so the man who gives them their orders must be able to inspire them to efforts which will, in turn stiffen the resolution and determination of the men to see the coup out. A coup d'état is not like a First World War slogging-match, it is more like a Second World War Commando raid – and the most successful raids were those carried out with determination, dash and élan. To these qualities in the commander must be added one more – intelligence.

FRIENDLY-ISH FORCES

We referred earlier to uncommitted troops whose inclination to do nothing makes them *de facto* supporters of the coup. Can we guarantee that they will do nothing? Consider the case of the Ugandan coup of 1971. The Army Chief of Staff, Brigadier Hussein, had been given orders by phone from Obote in Singapore to arrest Amin immediately on a variety of charges. Hussein was confident of the loyalty of much of the Ugandan Army and ordered trusted units to stand by for pre-emptive action against Amin (it was already known by this stage that Amin was planning a coup). One of the formations he counted on was the 2nd Brigade under Colonel Tito Okello, based at Masaka, some fifty miles south-west of the capital, Kampala. Okello was ordered to send a company group to Kampala, and then to await Hussein's further orders. The company group was detached from its guard duty at the Magamaga Ordnance Depot, some 30 miles away from Kampala, but by the time they got to their rendezvous, Amin's coup was under way and there was nobody present to give them any orders.

The coup took place on the night of Sunday, 25 January 1971. Okello's company arrived in Kampala some time after midnight; Okello waited until 10.30 the following morning – that is, Monday the 26th – before sending a second, section-strength, patrol up the road from Masaka to Kampala to see what was happening. After meeting some of Amin's troops, the section, and a reinforced platoon sent out later on, withdrew and set up an ambush which was dismantled on the Wednesday night. Despite transport shortages, Okello had not considered it necessary to comandeer local trucks and buses to move his men up to Kampala – he did not think the situation serious enough! He had been ordered by Hussein to await further instructions and, despite the lengthy silence from his superior, proceeded to do exactly that. In Okello's defence it must be said that the coup actually began when he and most of the other senior officers in the Ugandan Army were returning home from an officers' conference convened by Hussein in Kampala. Mutinies broke out in a majority of units in their commanders' absence and Okello had enormous difficulty in raising other formations as a result.

The picture is one of confusion, compounded by poor communications and personal fright. Okello was a loyal enough soldier (he escaped from Uganda and refused to serve under Amin), but a very ordinary one. Given similar conditions of confusion and fear, one could expect other commanders to do exactly the same thing, especially in the army of a country which is heavily polarized between supporters of the head of state and his enemies. It is a bleak fact of life that opinion in most armies does not run high enough for a majority of senior soldiers to take sides in a dispute. That old soldier, Sir Bernard Fergusson, once said: 'Ten per cent of the troops will fight, ten per cent will run away, and the rest will follow whichever group is making the most noise.' He admits to having over-simplified the case somewhat, but in broad terms he is absolutely correct and the trick, for the plotter, is to ensure that the ten per cent component which the rest of the army eventually follows is his own.

9
EXECUTION
The Pangea Plot

In the previous Chapters I have illustrated various points by referring to coups d'état which have taken place in the past and of which certain aspects are more or less reliably documented. I have also introduced a fictitious country, Gondwanaland, whose capital, Pangea, has served as a sort of classroom for the trainee coup plotter. Where reliably documented facts from real coups d'état have been scarce or non-existent, I have used Pangea as a sort of model upon which to develop various lines of thought. It is now time to draw these disparate strands together into a realistic and coherent whole, building upon what we have studied earlier. What now follows is fiction.

'The political background to the coup d'état which took place in Pangea on 31 June 1987 concerns us only in as much as it generated a fairly typical response from elements of the military and from the political opposition. The President was halfway through his second consecutive five-year term, but growing more unpopular by the day. The political opposition was so fragmented that the previous election had proved a disaster for them, notwithstanding the fact that the ruling party no longer enjoyed an overall majority in either house in Gondwanaland's bicameral parliamentary system.

It would be possible to lay too strong an emphasis on some of Gondwanaland's social problems in this context. True, the two major tribal groups, the Arianites and the Salaamites, were very different in both ethnic and religious terms, but this had never been a problem before. The trigger for this particular coup was created, ironically enough, by the President himself. He was a member of the smaller of the two tribes and the first ever to be elected President. The man had a chip on his shoulder; he had carried it through law school and his early political career. When he finally reached high office he let it get the better of him and he acquired a reputation for corruption and graft which was quite unique in the political history of twentieth-century Gondwanaland.

His political colour hardly worried the armed forces. What did worry them was the President's blatant nepotism; he had a large, extended family and was not above putting distant cousins and their friends and relations into political appointments. Even worse, he created a tribal problem where none had existed by excluding Salaamites from high office. His presidential style offended people and his fiscal policies frightened them. Not only were his economic theories at best contentious, but graft and patronage flourished during his presidency and the resulting distortions in the economic picture became embarrassing.

The last straw came when a contract which the Army had signed for the building of an ammunition factory was overturned by the President himself. The builder lost a great deal of money, the Army lost a good friend and much time was wasted while the President found another contractor more to his liking. The new contractor duly appeared and the Army was instructed to accept his terms – even though the cost of this contract would be nearly 100 per cent greater. It was an open secret that the President would pocket a huge commission on this deal while the Army's training budget for the next four years would be severely depleted to pay for this unwanted plant. The Joint Chiefs of Staff were furious.

As soon as they began grumbling the President asserted his authority. Typically, he over-reacted, sacking the Chief of the General Staff (CGS) and replacing him with a distant cousin who was promoted to General overnight. The Chief of the Defence Staff

(CDS), the senior General, spoke to one of his immediate subordinates, the Chief of the Naval Staff, who in turn spoke to his good friend the Flag Officer, Naval Air Command, who spoke earnestly to his uncle, the leader of the main opposition party, the Gondwana United Treaty Party (GUT). The plotting began.

There was never any suggestion that the armed forces would share power with any of the opposition parties – at least, not immediately; but the fighting men knew also that they were not equipped to run Gondwanaland by themselves. Their intention was simply to displace the President and his immediate hangers-on and rule by decree for long enough to allow the opposition parties to get their act together and form a caretaker government for the few weeks needed to prepare corruption charges on which to try the ex-President.

The Flag Officer, Naval Air Command (FONAC) mentioned none of this to his uncle. He merely inquired whether there was any real chance of the President's being defeated at the next election. Like most senior politicians the GUT leader was a realist and had to tell his favourite nephew, sadly, 'No.' When FONAC reported back to the CDS, the decision to mount a coup d'état was taken.

There was one major problem. The Chief of the General Staff (CGS) would be violently opposed to such a move, while the Chief of the Air Staff (CAS) was known to be ambivalent. Furthermore, both of these men were members of the same tribe, the Arianites, as were a large proportion of both the Army and the Air Force. Indeed, the Tectonic Knights were recruited exclusively from among the Arianites who, for all the President's personal faults, were courageous fighters and fine soldiers, rather like the Gurkhas. There were also Arianite units stationed up-country on the sensitive border with Bundustan; some of these units could return to Pangea quite rapidly and the prospect of civil war was not one which the CDS faced with equanimity.

The CDS had to weigh a number of contradictory factors before he could make a plan. The first of these was the size of force necessary simply to take Pangea and subdue it. The second was the ethnic breakdown of his forces. As mentioned earlier, there had never been a tribal problem in Gondwanaland. The two tribes had always got along fairly well and, until the election of the incumbent President, there had never been any suggestion that the recent past contained any history of discrimination against the Arianites. Now, however, the people had become polarized to a certain degree, and the tension under which the social fabric of both civilians and military had been placed was clearly evident. Would the armed forces break up into tribal factions after a coup d'état against an Arianite President?

There was no easy answer to this question and the CDS decided that careful presentation of his case to the people, along with the absolute minimum of bloodshed, would serve to hold the country together in the immediate aftermath of the coup, while some sort of normality was being restored. But he still did not know who would carry it out.

The Tectonic Knights could be written off immediately. They were the Presidential Guard and had been hand-picked for the job. They would represent the most immediate and direct resistance to any coup in Pangea. The Army HQ at Tel-el-Salaam had too high a proportion of Arianite political appointees to be a fertile breeding-ground for coup supporters. Nevertheless, there were enough sensible, objective staff officers of both tribes at Army HQ to make it possible for the garrison there to be neutralized. The Ruineck Garrison? Here the CDS paused in his deliberations. The 1st Armoured Brigade was in residence at Ruineck and was composed almost entirely of Salaamites. Who was their commander? Brigadier ben-Becula? The CDS had appointed him personally – he was a good soldier, but not a man whom the CDS knew intimately. Who was the second-in-command? Colonel ben-Lawers. The CDS didn't know him either, except by reputation; he was a high-flyer, ambitious and highly competent. The CDS rang for his ADC and asked for the personnel files on these two officers.

As it turned out, the ADC had been a classmate of the Colonel's at Staff College and knew him well. Their wives met regularly and the two men occasionally went hunting together in the mountains south of Pangea. The CDS decided to take his ADC (a Salaamite also) into his confidence and asked him to sound out this Colonel.

Two weeks later the ADC reported back. Colonel ben-Lawers thought it was time that something was done about the President or they would be saddled with him for the rest of their (and his) lives. The Colonel was fairly certain that Brigadier ben-Becula felt the same, but couldn't be entirely sure. The CDS ordered the Brigadier to be investigated in depth; while this was being done he, the CDS, would get on with his strategic planning.

The planning of the coup would be critical. A bloodless coup d'état is a product of timing, surprise, general acquiescence on the part of the population, and the presentation to the out-going Head of State of a *fait accompli.* The CDS couldn't be entirely certain whether the majority of elected representatives in the two Houses of Parliament would accept a coup d'état, or denounce it and rally support against it. Notwithstanding the fact that here was a hung Parliament in the Lower House and something close to chaos in the Upper, would the opposition take his part or the President's? Or would they remain sternly constitutionalist and condemn the coup regardless of their own personal feelings?

The CDS didn't know the answers to these questions and the GUT leader was no great help. When questioned obliquely on this (to him) academic problem he said that, at best, he could guarantee one-third support in the Lower House for a coup and about three-eighths in the Upper. He couldn't speak for the other parties although he knew their leaders well enough.

Should the coup be mounted while Parliament was in recess and the politicians scattered to their various constituencies? Could a coup survive the outrage many of them would feel if he mounted it while they were actually in session? He didn't know. Besides, at this stage he had so little information on which to work that he ignored the problem for the time being.

The major problem, the one around which the entire coup revolved, was that of seizing the President and his chief lieutenants. The President was well guarded, as were his cabinet ministers, and the CDS was worried that an attempted abduction might end up in a shoot-out resulting in the target's accidental death. Whatever the truth of the matter, such a death would inevitably receive a bad Press both at home and overseas and help to inflame opposition to the post-coup government. He didn't want Gondwanaland to suffer as had Chile from inexact and selective reporting of the post-coup situation so this problem occupied much of his spare time.

The CDS was lucky in one respect. A trusted member of his staff was a former commander of the Gondwanaland Army's Para-Commando Regiment which provided the country's anti-terrorist forces. He could be relied upon to find a way round government security – after all, he had literally written the manual.

At this point the magazine *Rumour Control* (a sort of Pangean *Private Eye* or *Canard Enchainé*) came to the CDS's aid. One of its journalists had managed to lay hands on a document proving the President's complicity in the ammunition-manufacturing contract, and the size of the commission the President was getting from the successful contractor. The Minister of Defence (one of the President's most trusted colleagues) clamped a D-notice (official request of news editors not to publish item) on the document forbidding its publication on grounds of national security. A circulated memo to this effect landed on the CDS's desk and sparked off an interesting train of thought in his Byzantine mind. Acting on his own authority, he sent the ex-Para-Commando staff officer down to the journal's office with orders to get hold of the document – discreetly. The officer did so by the simple expedient of breaking in by night and blowing open the editor's safe. Both the editor and the security police personnel who were sent next day to bring the document back to the Ministry of Defence were somewhat surprised to find the safe blown and the document gone.

Meanwhile, Brigadier ben-Becula had been vetted by his second-in-command and pronounced safe. The CDS invited ben-Becula down to his office in the Ministry of Defence and, after a short, routine discussion of mundane garrison matters, took him out for a walk in one of the city centre parks. Far from prying eyes, the CDS offered

9. The Pangea Coup: Command Structure

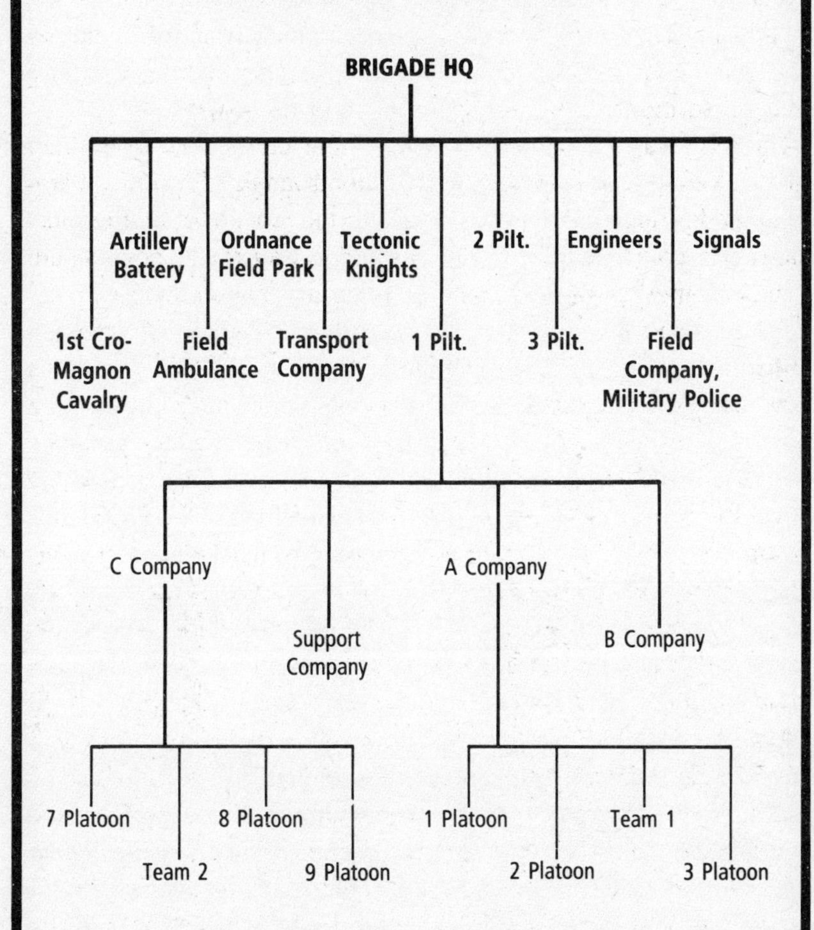

The Pangea Coup: command structure of that part of the main force (1 PILT battalion group) tasked with 'taking out' west-central Pangea and the area around Olduvai railway station. Note how two convert teams – Team 1 and Team 2 – are part of A and C companies respectively of 1 PILT for administrative purposes although during the early part of the Assault Phase there may be no direct contact between them and the companies concerned except by radio.

ben-Becula operational command of the coup, in which his brigade would play the major part. Ben-Becula agreed without hesitation and left immediately to begin his planning. Before he left the CDS warned ben-Becula that they couldn't afford to be seen together and so any liaison should be between the ADC and Colonel ben-Lawers.

The Para-Commando officer was charged with two tasks: first, to assemble a team of experts who could carry out covert operations in advance of the coup; secondly, to feed to the Press such titbits of salacious gossip as entered the Ministry of Defence – graft, corruption, greed and so on – involving the President and his cabinet. As part of his duties he had already prepared a governmental communications ORBAT which detailed the locations and interfaces of all types of communications equipment used routinely or in an emergency by the civil service, the various ministries, the Presidential office, and the armed forces. This appreciation naturally included a detailed outline of civil communications, but not the electronic media. On his own initiative, he prepared a staff paper on the electronic media which he was careful to classify at just low enough a level not to arouse suspicion in the Ministry of Defence. Finally, this energetic officer arranged for copies of all Police and Gendarmerie contingency plans (including protection of VIPs) to be filed in the Ministry of Defence, 'to improve co-operation and liaison between government agencies', as he put it.

One of FONAC's main tasks was to get from his uncle any information that he could on the real centres of power within the government and ruling party. Politicians are tremendous gossips and he was able to do this at a series of dinner-parties in fashionable south-side homes. When prodded in the right direction the GUT leader was only too happy to show off his knowledge of constitutional affairs and more especially his inside knowledge of the government. The gossip was scurrilous but essentially true and FONAC was able, after only a couple of weeks, to present the CDS with a list of personalities who must be neutralized during the Assault Phase of the coup. The CDS divided these people into two groups. One of them, composed of the less important figures, he assigned to the 1st

Armoured Brigade; the second, including the most heavily protected, he assigned to his Para-Commando officer as targets for the covert teams.

While the CDS was deliberating, Brigadier ben-Becula was having problems of his own. He had to ensure that either his battalion commanders or their second-in-commands would be available to lead the three infantry battalions under his command during the coup. He had to be equally sure of the commanders or their deputies in the artillery and armoured regiments under his command, while heads of department in the supporting arms had to be sounded out. It was a nightmarish task, given the recent and sudden tribal polarization of Gondwanaland; one of his heads of department (the senior engineer) was an Arianite known for his partisan views on the tribal problem. Brigadier ben-Becula had, somehow, to prevent word of the coup getting to the Arianite sappers and their commanding officer while ensuring that planning went ahead without delays.

He did this by 'volunteering' his sappers for a public works programme deep in the heart of Arianite country to the south of Pangea where, he knew, they would be virtually cut off from normal brigade gossip, building farm tracks in a remote, mountainous part of Gondwanaland. The sapper rear party at Ruineck was commanded by a grizzled major, nearing pensionable age, who happened to be an old friend of the CO of 1 PILT and, like him, an old-fashioned Salaamite.

These two officers, having been sounded out by Colonel ben-Lawers, were taken into his confidence and warned on pain of death to say nothing to anybody. The sapper officer proved invaluable, in fact, in reorganizing the engineer stores at Ruineck in preparation for the coup; he made sure that there would be no shortage of anti-tank obstacles, barbed wire and other stores on the day when they would be needed. He also had the small section under his command trained as operators of bulldozers and heavy plant – ostensibly to keep them busy.

The CO of 1 PILT was told in very broad terms what was afoot and told to do plenty of sightseeing in the west end of Pangea. He was also told to practise his men in FIBUA – Fighting in Built-up Areas – and carry out a couple of Command Post Exercises (CPXs) to get his headquarters and those of his subordinate company commanders up to speed in the rapid passing of orders and dissemination of information both up and down the chain of command.

Back at the Ministry of Defence the CDS was watching his plans fall into place. Some of the vital information picked up by his Para-Commando officer (a Lieutenant-Colonel ben-Macdhui) had been passed on to Brigadier ben-Becula, while that officer was busy recruiting covert teams to take out some of the Priority A targets. In this he had problems. The Para-Commando Regiment was a multi-racial force composed of thorough professionals who, nevertheless, had either Salaamite or Arianite affiliations of varying strength. Lieutenant-Colonel ben-Macdhui got around this problem by approaching known Salaamite partisans among the Para-Commandos, the Police and the Gendarmerie, along with recently retired Para-Commando officers and NCOs who would be sympathetic to the idea of a coup. Contact with these men, as with all key personnel among the plotters, was made by word of mouth and a competent, highly skilled force was gradually assembled of men who knew Pangea like the backs of their hands or who knew more about VIP security than the average Pangea constable was likely to realize existed.

The main problem, that of 'taking out' the President, had not yet been solved, but windows of opportunity were beginning to open, and some of these looked quite promising. In early March of that year, the presidential palace had released details of the Head of State's programme for the coming twelve months; by mid-April the CDS was pencilling-in potential dates for a coup. There were no overseas visits planned before the end of the year, which was a pity, and the State Opening of Parliament had already passed; but one particular date caught the attention of ben-Macdhui. This was National Day, 31 June, when it was known that all the human targets would be concentrated in Pangea for the parade and celebrations. So, too, would the Tectonic Knights but, as ben-Macdhui explained, this could work in the plotters' favour.

His plan, as explained to the CDS, was disarmingly simple. The Knights would spend so long planning and rehearsing for the National Day parade that, after it was over, they would be let off the hook for the night and most of the regiment would be so drunk that they wouldn't know that a coup was in progress, far less be able to prevent it. Mentally marking down ben-Macdhui as a dangerous man, the CDS agreed. Foreign ambassadors and members of the Gondwanaland Establishment would be at the official reception after the parade which normally ended by about 21.00 hrs, after which the President traditionally had dinner with his cabinet in the presidential palace. The streets would be clear and the President would be alone by midnight. The majority of human targets would by then be at home, packaged neatly for abduction.

The CDS agreed, 31 June it would be. The question was: How? Here, Brigadier ben-Becula came up with what turned out to be part of the solution: live-firing exercises. It was the Gondwanaland Army's exercise season but, due to the restrictions in training budget imposed by the ammunition manufacturing deal, there would be very few large-scale exercises. On the other hand there was a vast quantity of ageing ammunition waiting to be used in anticipation of the new plant coming on stream. The 1st Armoured Brigade could indent for large stocks of live ammunition for training on the ranges south of Pangea. The training value of such an exercise would be enormous and any ammunition not used need not be returned to store, need it? All it would take would be a bit of, um, creative accounting.

Another piece of the jigsaw fell into place when the CDS himself proposed returning the stolen document to *Rumour Control*'s editor with an instruction to print it as soon as possible, and to hell with D-notices. If this could be done a few days in advance of the National Day celebrations, the public outcry would be enough to justify the presence on the streets of extra troops and police in order to keep the crowd under control. In all the confusion nobody would notice the extra military activity leading up to the coup that night.

All that remained was to find a foolproof plan for abducting the President and his senior lieutenants either during or shortly after the

National Day dinner at the presidential palace. The commander of the 3 PILT signals platoon provided another part of the answer. One of his earlier assignments had been to the communications staff of the presidential command post, deep in the bowels of the Citadel. He knew the physical location of every piece of communications equipment in the palace, the citadel and between the two, and how they connected. Working with ben-Macdhui he was able to draw up a simple plan for cutting telephone cables, cutting down radio antennae and breaking up microwave dishes at both ends of the digital data link between the Citadel and the Army Headquarters at Tel-el-Salaam. With the main elements of presidential control decoupled, the President himself and the Citadel could be secured comparatively easily.

It was the CDS who slipped the last piece of the jigsaw into place. After the National Day dinner at the presidential palace, he would enter the palace himself accompanied by a small staff. He would bluff his way towards the state apartments by saying that an emergency was in progress and that he needed to talk immediately to the President. At the right moment he and his staff would pull out concealed pistols and round up the President and his personal staff while a company from 3 PILT would enter the palace and secure it. The Presidential family would be confined to quarters while the politicians would be locked in the noisome cellars.

While all this planning had been going on, the various units of the 1st Armoured Brigade were going through the motions of a series of live-firing exercises down at Bighorn Ranges. All the brigade weapons from pistols to artillery pieces were fired and the troops, many of whom had fired live ammunition only during basic training, were exhilarated to be able to use almost unlimited amounts of ammunition and learn to be real soldiers. The extensive FIBUA training undergone by most of the infantry was tremendous fun, and most thought that this was a consolation prize for having had their major field training exercises curtailed for financial reasons. Even the CGS himself came down to do his annual personal weapon test (for the first time in several years) and took the chance, in the spring

10. Gondwanaland Army Command Structure, Pangea District

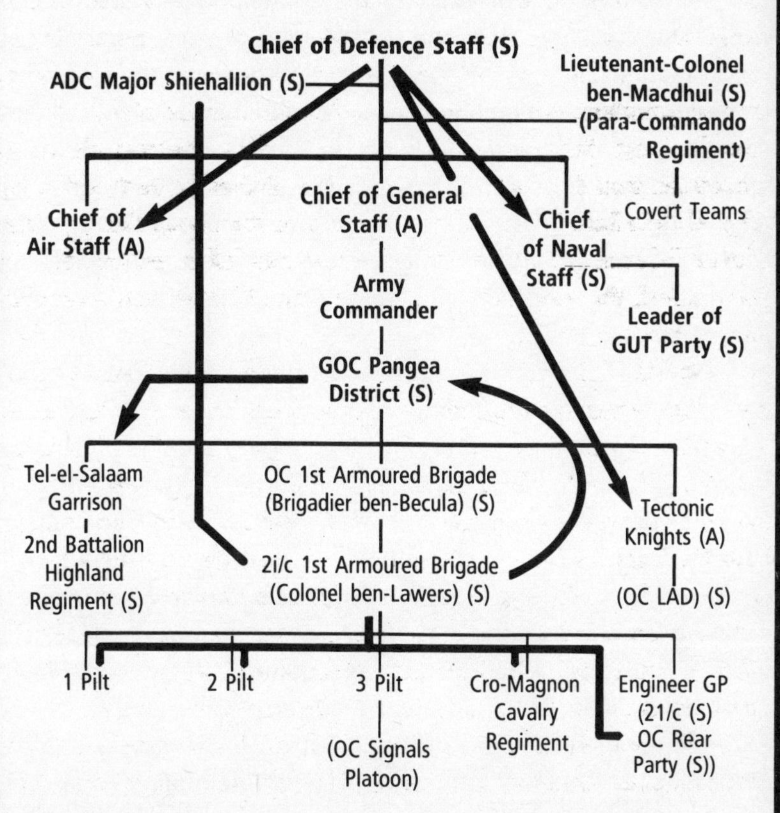

This diagram shows the command structure of the Gondwanaland Army in the region surrounding Pangea. (S) denotes Salaamite sympathies and (A) Arianite. The broken lines denote the flow of information and orders, and the order in which contacts were made, among the plotters. Thus it will be seen that although the direction for the coup came from the very top – from the Chief of the Defence Staff – three of the most important characters in the entire enterprise were his ex-Para-Commando staff officer, Lieutenant-Colonel ben-Macdhui, second in command of the 1st Armoured Brigade, Colonel ben-Lawers, and the CDS's aide de camp, Major Shiehallion. Note how comparatively junior officers carried out much of the leg-work, by-passing Arianite or uncommitted superiors.

sunshine, to fire as many different infantry weapons as he could during the single day he was there. Brigadier ben-Becula breathed a sigh of relief when it became clear that the CGS would not be spending the night in the Bighorn officers' mess – those of his officers who knew what was afoot were getting a little restive and he feared an indiscretion.

As May became June and National Day drew near, secretaries sunbathing during lunch-hour in the gardens below the Citadel could hear the drill sergeants putting the Tectonic Knights through their paces in preparation for the big day. The CDS went to watch, partly because it was his duty, but more especially because the commander of the Mechanical Engineers' Light Aid Detatchment (LAD) had turned out to be a useful mole among the Knights. He was a Salaamite, a tough little captain with a brilliant career ahead of him as a used car salesman, and with no respect for authority. The CDS asked to be shown the armoured vehicle garage, recently hewn out of the rock, and insisted on walking there the long way, past the Knights' armoury. The Captain understood, and chattered away nonchalantly about the appalling security inside the Citadel's walls, and the vulnerability of the Knights to somebody with a tube of 'super-glue'. When the CDS asked what he meant, the Captain explained.

All it would take, he reckoned, was one man with a tube of 'super-glue' to seal the locks on the armoury and garage doors, and to jam the key-switches in their security alarms, and the Knights would have no weapons and no vehicles. Without these, the ammunition, stored near the main gates in a secure compound, would be useless. The CDS agreed and, five days later, the Captain received, by mail to his home address, five large tubes of glue.

The Army Headquarters at Tel-el-Salaam remained something of a problem. Next to the Tectonic Knights, the armoured brigade there was best placed to intervene in the coup. The problem was, as the CDS explained to ben-Becula, that he couldn't take anybody there into his confidence, not even the Salaamite officers; the security risk with so many senior Arianites about was too great. The Brigadier considered this problem, then proposed sending ben-Lawers down there on the evening of National Day to pass the news on to selected Salaamite officers who could be relied on to immobilize the garrison and arrest any senior Arianites who tried to interfere. It was the best idea anybody could come up with and the CDS reluctantly agreed, mentally noting that correct presentation of this particular coup was going to be vital if the entire Arianite component of the armed forces was not to rise up and start a civil war. What he really needed was a senior Arianite beside him who could give the lie to inevitable tribalistic rumours. Would the CAS play ball?

On 29 June the leaked document was published by *Rumour Control* amid intense excitement. The editor was promptly arrested and his offices shut down, but the national Press had already picked up the story, and banner headlines on the 30th proclaimed the President's duplicity. The CDS was interviewed but said very little in an outward show of loyalty to his paymaster. The Minister of Defence was hounded though the Upper House in Parliament and returned home that night pale and shaking. While the President maintained a bland silence behind the wrought-iron gates of the palace, the CGS went on TV to give a limp explanation of the situation. The CDS, Chief of the Naval Staff and CAS sat together in the CDS's office at lunchtime on the 30th, watching the CGS squirm under the glare of Gondwanaland Television's elder statesman, a highly experienced reporter and interviewer who had been known to wring tears from strong men. The CAS shook his head in disgust and made some offensive remark about his fellow tribesmen in general and the CGS and President in particular. The CDS picked up this point and questioned the CAS closely. Would he like to see the President go? Yes, replied the CAS, but he couldn't see how the President could be made to go without using force.

The CDS leant forward earnestly and looked the CAS in the eyes. 'Would you use force, if necessary?,' he asked. The CDS stared at the carpet for a second then looked up to meet the CDS's eye. 'Yes I would, but I don't want any bloodshed,' he replied. The CDS led him out into the park near the Ministry of Defence and told him what was happening. He decided that he should tell the CAS the whole story as he didn't want any unpleasant revelations after the coup destroying what was, at the moment, a fragile but very necessary unity. The CAS was incensed to discover that plotting had been going on behind his back, but resigned himself to the fact that the coup was going to happen in any case and that for a variety of reasons it would be best for the country and his service if he took part himself. As he sat down at his desk after this walk, he crossed himself.

The Sappers were back at Ruineck, none the wiser about the coup and disgruntled that they were going to miss the parade this year. Their commander went on leave almost as soon as he returned to barracks, to the delight and relief of ben-Becula. The Sapper second-in-command was a reliable young officer who could be taken into the Brigadier's confidence and, in the evening of 30 June, he was briefed on his role and specialist tasks for the next day.

National Day began as it ended, dry and clear without a breath of wind. The Parade began at 11.00 sharp, the Tectonic Knights' armoured cars leading a mounted detachment, then 1 PILT and a squadron of the Cro-Magnon Cavalry's M-48 tanks, out of the Citadel, down Hospital Hill towards the palace, along ben-Mhor Avenue facing the Citadel and back up Jurassic Hill. Although the route was lined with flags and bunting, and the crowds were large, there was comparative silence except for the Knights' pipers, skirling their hearts out at the front of the column. The President and Chiefs of Staff arrived on the saluting base outside the palace to a stony silence from the crowd who watched, grim-faced, as the men and machines passed, then began to jeer and shout catcalls at the President. He ignored them, and didn't notice that the CAS's hands were shaking ever so slightly as he led the Joint Chiefs back to their official cars.

As soon as the parade returned to the Citadel, all personnel from the 1st Armoured Brigade were returned to Ruineck. The officers stayed to eat their customary National Day lunch in the Citadel's ceremonial hall; the mood there was unusually subdued – the Knights' CO put it down to the sullen crowd and the dampening effect of the eerie silence as the parade marched through the city. As soon as lunch was over the guests made their excuses and left.

Due to the security precautions surrounding the parade, nobody outside took any notice of the extra security at the gates of Ruineck Barracks. Nobody noticed, therefore, that the officers changed straight into combat kit and assembled in the dining-room of their Mess for an address by the Brigadier. As soon as they knew what was afoot, two subalterns tried to escape. They were arrested and confined in the ante-room under armed guard. The civilian Mess staff had been given the day off as soon as breakfast was over.

The CDS arrived at Ruineck shortly after 16.00 hrs to brief the Brigadier and his immediate subordinates. With him were Lieutenant-Colonel ben-Macdhui and his ADC, Major Shiehallion. The briefing was short and to the point. There was going to be a coup d'état that night; all units from 1st Armoured were to take part and there would be, literally, a new dawn in the history of Gondwanaland. The CDS kept it brief and workmanlike. He knew the effect that he had on his subordinates; he was inspiring, persuasive and capable of instilling tremendous enthusiasm and loyalty in his men, and he gave it everything he had. The result, when he stopped speaking, was a buzz of excited conversation the equivalent under these circumstances of a resounding cheer. There was no doubt that the coup would succeed and, as he led Brigadier ben-Becula into the latter's office to give him his final orders, the CDS warned that the psychological momentum must be maintained at all costs.

There had been no changes in the plan agreed between the CDS and Brigadier ben-Becula, but the CDS warned him not to expect too much from ben-Lawers' mission to Tel-el-Salaam. Just in case the worst happened, he said, the 1st Armoured Brigade should be prepared for a nasty fight out to the west of Pangea. The Brigadier was unruffled. He had already made provision for the Cro-Magnon Recce Troop to take up position on the western perimeter of the airport to watch out for any signs of resistance, with two squadrons of tanks sited hull-down on a line running north-south along the eastern perimeter to take care of the Tel-el-Salaam garrison. In effect, he had placed an armour-heavy battle group in a blocking position between Pangea and Tel-el-Salaam; this battle group, however, had absorbed most of the brigade's infantry support weapons, leaving only a few mortars and TOW missiles guarding the southern approaches to the city.

The CDS handed over the brigade's written orders (a single sheet of foolscap, covered in hand-written script), reminded the Brigadier to watch out for covert parties operating in Pangea, and left.

The Brigadier called an 'O' Group of his battalion commanders, senior staff officers and heads of department and gave his own orders less than an hour later. It was now 18.00 hrs.

Three hours later, the heads of department and battalion commanders had given their own orders to the men under their command; these were necessarily sketchy and each officer knew he was throwing a heavy burden on the junior NCOs he led, but there was no alternative. Better in this case the tight security which short notice represented than a long lead time and inevitable leaks.

At about this time the last guests were drifting away from the reception at the presidential palace. The pubs round the back of ben-Mhor Street were doing a roaring trade and the Tectonic Knights were completely finished as a fighting force from that moment on.

Lieutenant-Colonel ben-Macdhui dispatched the first covert teams from Ruineck at about 00.30 and these headed straight for their objectives. The CDS left the Ministry of Defence at about 00.45 and, with two Land Rovers full of armed troops, raced down to the presidential palace. He was not stopped at the gate and led his men straight to the side entrance to the palace used by troops on guard duty.

'Emergency!,' he yelled at the startled Orderly Sergeant. 'I must see the President, Which way?' The sergeant led him upstairs through the palace towards the state apartments where they were met by a tough-looking armed policeman. The CDS and his men kept their pistols concealed while the policemen checked their security passes, then they marched smartly down a corridor to a set of double doors at which the sergeant stopped.

'The President's in here sir,' he said. 'Wait in that room and I'll ask his private secretary to fetch him for you.' The unfortunate sergeant was pushed against the wall by one of the retinue and a pistol muzzle rammed into his mouth while the CDS opened the doors and marched in, pistol levelled. The President and his wife were in bed, asleep. As four other officers barged in, also with pistols, a single shot echoed down the corridor. One of the officers stuck his head cautiously round the door. The policeman had tried to draw his weapon on the seventh member of the party, but hadn't been quick enough. The shaken Orderly Sergeant was dragged into the room and ordered to sit in front of the fireplace. Before the CDS could speak there was a sudden flurry as the President pulled a pistol from under his pillow. Two of the officers fired simultaneously; one round hit the President in the stomach, flinging him back against the pillow, the other hit his wife in the shoulder. The CDS let out a sulphurous oath; he was no friend of the President but wounding him – perhaps killing him – and maltreating his wife would not do the cause any good.

Luckily, there was a medical officer attached to A Company 3 PILT – the CDS could hear their vehicles entering the palace courtyard now – and the couple would be looked after properly. While two of the officers ran down the corridor to round up the President's staff and his three daughters, the CDS gave orders that the President and his wife be taken immediately to the nearest hospital in a sealed ambulance and kept there, under tight security, until they recovered. Army medics, he insisted, should carry out any necessary treatment.

1 PILT left Ruineck barracks at about the same time as the CDS left the ministry. The rifle companies headed straight for the west end of Pangea while detachments from the mortar, anti-tank and machine-gun platoons went straight to the airport. There, at the main entrance, they were met by the commander of one of the covert parties which had already secured the control tower and switched off all the runway and landing lights. He ordered them to take up positions on a hill to the east and cover both main roads into the city, along with the

airport runways. The Air Force would be responsible for security inside the airport itself.

The rifle companies got to the bottom of Jurassic Hill at about 01.10 hrs, just in time to see the brilliant flash as the radio mast on top of the Citadel, which carried the antennae and microwave dishes, was destroyed by a second covert party. C Company had been detailed to seal off the western end of ben-Mhor Street and the bottom of Jurassic Hill, and set about fortifying this major road junction. B Company doubled the 500 metres towards the River Dean and then split up to defend the two road bridges which crossed it less than half a mile apart. A Company, with two platoons of impressed Ordnance Corps storemen under command, raced down the main road towards Olduvai railway station and had sealed it off within five minutes; one of its platoons, meanwhile, headed for the Georgian terrace in which the Foreign Minister and Prime Minister lived. Within half an hour western Pangea was secure. The battalion's CO informed Brigadier ben-Becula at his headquarters that his Priority A targets had been taken. While a single platoon from A Company remained at the station to stiffen the storemen guarding it, two other platoons fanned out through the area to place the Trade Unions HQ under guard and to run through a series of other minor tasks.

The Brigadier was already in the Citadel. One of the covert groups had rushed the guards at the main gate – fortunately, like ceremonial guards everywhere, these were not armed with live ammunition and hadn't had time to inform the guardroom that they were under attack – and had sprinted for the radio mast up on the Citadel's roof. Less than five minutes later A Company of 2 PILT had entered the Citadel and, in the confusion, shot two of their own men whom they thought were armed Tectonic Knights making a stand near the AFV garage. It took another ten minutes for the signals group attached to ben-Becula's headquarters party to rig up HF and VHF antennas in place of the destroyed ones, and the Brigadier was able to move into the Knights' CO's office and set up his own command post. He was joined some half an hour later by the CDS who remained at the Citadel for the remainder of the night.

Another covert team had already taken up position outside the Gondwanaland Television Studios while the President was being arrested. They saw the flash of the Citadel's radio mast going up, but they didn't go into action until they heard the shots as the troops in the Citadel opened fire on one another. Using CS gas grenades and British Royal-Ordnance-built Arwen anti-riot guns, they stormed into the building, firing baton rounds over the heads of terrified technicians and broadcasters. They had already been briefed on the location of the sound-proof studio and control room from which the current late-night film was being broadcast, and they succeeded in securing the entire facility without word getting out to the viewing public that a coup was in progress. The film played itself out and a continuity announcer with a gun at his head read out the station's normal good night message before shutting down.

The radio station was not so easy to shut down quietly. For one thing, it broadcast all night. For another, the studio used by the all-night disc-jockey wasn't sound-proof enough to allow any shooting during the assault. Lieutenant-Colonel ben-Macdhui decided to ignore the studio and take out the broadcast antennas instead, and a covert team was detailed to do this. The antennas complex, in fact, remained unharmed – the thick, coaxial cables leading to it were cut by a linear explosive charge – and a disgruntled and rather frightened radio engineer was dragged out of his bed in the middle of the night to make the necessary repairs by morning. In the meantime, the covert team had been able to secure the radio station at their leisure.

The city's three main telephone exchanges were under the control of one or other of the covert teams almost from the moment the CDS entered the presidential palace, and communications between Pangea and the provinces, and within Pangea itself, were efficiently and quietly strangled. As soon as they were secure the exchanges and broadcasting studios came under control of units of the 1st Armoured Brigade while the covert teams reported back to the Citadel. There, all was quiet. The Knights, taken completely by surprise, had given up with poor grace, but a realistic appreciation of their own weakness. Those Knights still down in the town filtered back up the hill and, drunk as many of them were, it wasn't difficult to place them under guard in the Citadel's ancient dungeons. By now, those that had got away were in no position to reverse the coup.

Colonel ben-Lawers had spent a most agreeable evening at Tel-el-Salaam. He had a number of friends there, and had enjoyed an excellent dinner with them in the historic house which had become their Mess. After dinner he and some of his Salaamite colleagues had retired to the ante-room where, after making sure nobody was within earshot, he told them what was happening. The senior Salaamite there was a high-flying Major-General (the GOC, Pangea District, in fact) with whom ben-Lawers had family ties, and the Colonel played on his vanity by presenting an impassioned (and quite impromptu) plea for assistance from, he said, the CDS. He explained the need for secrecy, said said how confident the CDS was that he would understand, and requested most earnestly the General's help in making sure the coup succeeded. Keeping Tel-el-Salaam buttoned up, assured the Colonel, was one of the most critical elements of the entire coup. Only the Major-General could ensure this.

The General wasted no time. Colonel ben-Lawers had read his man correctly and the GOC didn't disappoint him. He reasoned that there was no time to be wasted explaining things to his officers, and then arresting those members of his staff – and any of his superiors – who turned out to be dissenting Arianites. All he could do was hit the panic button, assume immediate command of the Army HQ and give himself wide powers; in the confusion nobody would know what he was up to and by the time anyone tumbled to the fact, it would be too late. Colonel ben-Lawers would have preferred the coup to have taken place over the weekend when most of the troops would have been off the base. On the other hand, there were plenty of good men available who would make a positive contribution to its success, so he decided that he shouldn't complain.

The GOC took the same view. The first thing he did was to have a quiet word with his chief of staff, who had joined them after dinner, and order him to put an armed – Salaamite – guard on the garrison armoury and magazine. He then ordered a platoon of troops to 'go like hell' for the ordnance depot, 10km south of Tel-el-Salaam, in case the CDS's men hadn't got there first. The last thing he wanted was 2,000 tonnes of rifle, artillery and tank ammunition falling into the wrong hands.

The Army Commander was a crusty Salaamite of the old school who lived in a house within the Tel-el-Salaam perimeter but close to the airport. He had to know what was going on, but the GOC wanted to restrict his freedom of manoeuvre in case the old boy was too constitutionally minded to allow the coup to go ahead. Colonel ben-Lawers was ordered to telephone him from the main switchboard inside the guardroom, tell him there was a major emergency in progress and that he should get to his headquarters as soon as possible. Ben-Lawers would then shut down the switchboard and so prevent all telephone traffic into and out of Tel-el-Salaam. Were there any all-Salaamite units at Tel-el-Salaam? The Colonel knew there were and suggested strongly that the unit concerned – the 2nd Battalion, The Highland Regiment – should be mobilized and ordered to guard both the main gates and the headquarters itself.

'What about Arianite officers at the HQ?,' asked the GOC. The Colonel produced a list of known Arianites: 'Let me have the Highlanders' Recce Platoon for half an hour and I'll roll 'em all up, sir.' The GOC nodded and, a few minutes later, the arrests began. The Army Commander, reacting with commendable speed, was inside headquarters within ten minutes, dressed in casual clothes but wearing his hat with the gold braid and scarlet band. The GOC gave him a carefully edited version of the truth. A coup d'état was imminent in Pangea; nobody knew who was behind it but there seemed to be an Arianite flavour to the whole thing. Communications with the Citadel, Ministry of Defence and presidential palace had been cut off and there was no reply from Ruineck Barracks. He had placed the Highlanders on alert and sealed off the camp.

There was little else either he or the Army Commander could do. Colonel ben-Lawers reported back from his sweep through the camp and volunteered to take a fighting patrol into Pangea to find out what was happening, but was told that he might be too valuable in Tel-el-

Salaam; if necessary, he might have to negotiate with renegades from Ruineck or lead a force up there himself. The Highlanders' Recce Platoon, with a rifle company in support, was ordered to make its way into Pangea at top speed to find out what was going on; in the meantime the Army commander wanted to interview the arrested Arianite officers. Carefully avoiding the shut-down switchboard, ben-Lawers led the Army Commander to the cells where the unfortunate Arianites were incarcerated. Not unnaturally, they denied all knowledge of the coup attempt. Unconvinced, the Army Commander decided to wait until the Highlanders had reported back and to keep his powder dry in the meantime.

Colonel ben-Lawers took a brave step at this stage. He pointed out, not unreasonably, that the coup might be an attempt by an Arianite minority to seize power; if this were the case, the Army's unity would probably suffer unnecessarily unless it was seen that loyal Arianite troops were involved in putting down the coup. He proposed taking an Arianite infantry company up to Ruineck and volunteering their service alongside the 1st Armoured Brigade as a show of army unity. The Army Commander reluctantly agreed, and within twenty minutes the convoy of trucks, led by ben-Lawers' staff car, all showing white flags (the Salaamite recognition signal) were racing across the city suburbs on a roundabout route to Ruineck.

Colonel ben-Lawers led the convoy deliberately into the southern portion of the Cro-Magnon defensive line and was stopped by a young troop sergeant who demanded to know who the hell he was. The Colonel identified himself quietly, stated that he had reinforcements and demanded the whereabouts of the regiment's commanding officer. He ordered the Arianites to wait in their vehicles while he conferred with the cavalryman's commander and, from the Cro-Magnon HQ's command post, succeeded in speaking to ben-Becula up at the Citadel. The Brigadier was relieved to hear ben-Lawers' news and ordered him to take the company down to the south-eastern part of the city, well away from Ruineck, the Citadel and the rest of the brigade, and leave them there for the time being. Then he was to report back to Tel-el-Salaam; by the time he got there the signallers should have rigged up a direct radio link with the Army HQ, and either the Army Commander would be in charge or he would be under guard with the GOC running the show.

It was two hours before ben-Lawers got back to Tel-el-Salaam, and when he arrived a white flag was just discernible, tugging gently at the guardroom flag pole in the first light of dawn. The Army Commander was still in charge. The CDS had told him the truth, but not the whole truth, over the radio. Nobody at Tel-el-Salaam, apart from ben-Lawers' immediate circle of friends and the GOC himself, knew the truth of the Colonel's involvement in the coup. The Army Commander explained to him what (he thought) had happened, patted him on the shoulder and commiserated gruffly with the Colonel's 'obvious' embarrassment at having been misled by 'that duplicitous swine the CDS', but congratulated him on his clear thinking and quick action which had saved the Arny from a most unpleasant internecine squabble. Besides, the country was better off without the President, though God alone knew what was going to happen now.

Colonel ben-Lawers had a fairly good idea what was going to happen; there would be an almighty row between the CDS and the Army Commander, followed either by the latter's resignation or by his early retirement within a few months. The Army's unity would be preserved, the unfortunate arrest of the Arianites at Tel-el-Salaam dismissed as the fog of war (or typical army inefficiency) and the CDS and Joint Chiefs of Staff would take over the country while the opposition parties put their house in order and tried to put together a worthwhile programme for the elections at the end of the year. Thank god the political parties weren't recruited along tribal lines, he thought.

Shortly before 06.00 hrs on 1 July, Colonel ben-Lawers decided to get some sleep. He'd done his bit, it had been a long night and he was getting too old for this sort of thing. As he drove from the Army HQ building to the Officers' Mess, he switched on the radio. It was Radio Pangea, broadcasting the pre-recorded tape which the CDS had prepared two – no, three days ago, now: 'The President of

Gondwanaland, that leech on the body politic, who has been enriching himself through corrupt political practices, has been overthrown by the country's armed forces working together in a spirit of national unity and reconstruction. Citizens are warned that martial law has been imposed on Gondwanaland and that they are to remain at home until further notice. The government of Gondwanaland is now the responsibility of the Chief of the Defence Staff and his subordinate chiefs of staff of the Army, Navy and Air Force . . .' The colonel switched off. So far, so good, he mused. Nobody killed that I know of, a nice neat little operation considering it was put together under a blanket. We even managed to scoop the BBC World Service. That must prove something. His last thought before going to sleep was: have they released *Rumour Control*'s editor yet?

10
AFTERMATH

'Then he waited, marshalling his thoughts and brooding over his still untested powers. For though he was master of the world, he was not quite sure what to do next.'

'But he would think of something.'

These words are the last in Arthur C. Clarke's science fiction classic, *2001 – A Space Odyssey*, and they are highly appropriate here because they encapsulate the very real problem facing the recently successful coup plotter: 'Now what?'

No military officer of any intelligence will claim to be able to run a country all by himself, or even to run a small part of the country, except perhaps the armed forces. It is a feature of military coups d'état down the ages that the military government which follows is not, in fact, a military government at all, but a surprisingly normal government given an unorthodox complexion by the presence in certain posts of officers from the armed forces.

When General Siwar al Dhahab deposed President Gaafar Mohamed El Nimeiri of the Sudan during the latter's absence in Washington in 1985, he was under no illusions as to his ability to rule the country himself. Instead, he told the people that he would be forming a committee of civilians and military personnel who would run the country under his control, and promised free and fair elections within the year. He was as good as his word. In Nigeria, successive periods of military rule have been characterized by soldiers, sailors and airmen running particular organizations or provinces through a secretariat of predominantly civilian personnel – civil servants mainly – in the full knowledge that their period of tenure is going to be limited. In both Nigeria and Ghana, after all, the military regimes have, at one stage or another, promised a return to civilian rule and have stuck by that promise.

The same holds true, broadly speaking, just about everywhere a coup has taken place. Military men, by their very nature, are not politicians or administrators, except in their own very narrow fields where their constituency is very different from that which they encounter in the outside world. A joint civil-military administration becomes the norm with the military ostentatiously in the ascendancy.

One mistake which a number of military regimes make, however, is to attempt to impose a martial frame of mind onto a civilian population, enforcing rigid discipline in some areas but quite ignoring their responsibilities in others. Senior military officers are soldiers by inclination, not by force. Their particular view of the world is coloured by their training, their experience (or, perhaps more accurately, their lack of experience of the civilian world with its vastly different mind-set) and whatever it is that makes them want to be soldiers at all. For soldiering is more than just a profession – it is a vocation, much like medicine, or teaching or the clergy. People who follow a vocation tend to make their view of the world conform to their perception of the vocation. For this reason alone soldiers tend to keep out of politics if they feel that the politicians are doing well enough without them. The army is the servant of the State; the State is not a playground for the army.

What happens, though, when this master-servant relationship becomes distorted or breaks down altogether? As often as not the result is a coup; but do the soldiers have any clear idea of what it is they are seeking? They may say they do, and explain their reasons for supplanting the government quite convincingly, but do they understand the nature of the power they will then hold? The answer to this question is probably, No.

It must be borne in mind that, whatever the reasons put forward for mounting a coup (and these may be honest – noble, even), self-interest has a great deal of say in what happens next. The clique that has seized power has set itself up as being indispensable to the country's general well-being and, even if a return to the former type of rule has been promised, the people must not be allowed to forget that this will occur only through the good offices of that clique. As we are talking here about coups d'état, let us take for granted that they result almost invariably in a military government. We can ignore, for these purposes, revolutionary coups.

No coup takes place in isolation. A Coup d'état has many causes, as we have seen, and the conditions which led to the coup taking place are unlikely to change overnight. Depending upon the part of the world in question, these conditions could include tribal problems (everywhere in Africa), religious problems (Iran, Sudan, Egypt), political bitterness and extreme polarization (Latin America), economic problems (everywhere) and bribery and corruption on a grand scale (most of the Third World). Most of these problems have their roots in the demographic and historical make-up of the country concerned. To say that a small clique of military men (and remember that professional soldiers are in a minority in all countries, due to a sense of vocation which is confined to only a small part of the population) can attack and solve these problems is fanciful in the extreme.

The military men know this. Very few soldiers have ever come to power promising a solution to all their country's problems; most of them make a feature of some problem which can be solved – corruption or economic malpractice – and promise only to try and restore a stable framework in which long-term solutions to other major problems can be worked out. A simple analogy might be that of a house with a leaky roof: the new government may pump the rain water out of the house, may even put a few sheets of flimsy plastic over the holes in the roof, but it is the responsibility of the householder to make permanent repairs to the structure. All the army can do is prevent the family from quarrelling and try to motivate them to find a satisfactory long-term solution.

A major problem facing any country which has suffered a coup d'état is that of precedent; it has happened once, it can happen again. A coup weakens the political institutions to a greater degree than any internecine strife in the civilian sector may have done before; it makes military rule a more or less acceptable norm. However, it can polarize public opinion against the military men; and when politicians feel strong enough to raise their heads above the constitutional parapet it is very often to make political capital out of an attack on the military. Thus any return to civilian rule will be flawed because the new generation of civilian politicians needs a context within which to operate and against which to react and the only context available is the one created by the military themselves.

The politicization of the military presents an enormous problem in the aftermath of a coup. Once an intelligent officer sees for himself how the country is run, and learns how to do it in even an imperfect way, he is in a position to make value judgements on the performance of a civilian government after the military has returned to barracks. If the civilians don't measure up to his own personal standards – and if he can make capital out of this shortfall – the prospect of another coup taking place cannot be ignored. Another problem, of course, is the formation of clicques within the armed forces resulting from the experience of government. Some will prefer one type of government, some another. An army divided against itself along party political lines is not a pretty sight; one fears that the army is having trouble in deciding for itself whether or not to continue supporting the government. The unique master-servant relationship between government and military has been destroyed; in any country the army must be the servant – slave, even – of government so far as morality and the legitimacy of that government allow. To make support for the government conditional on its political complexion, economic policy, or its attitude to the probability of green men living on Mars is to assume a praetorian stance which offers little to the country's social and political development.

Somebody one said, 'There are no bad soldiers, only bad officers.' Another over-simplification, but one which we can use here. Substitute the word 'governments' for 'officers'; we now begin to appreciate the nature, in the most basic terms of course, of civil-military relations. We have come almost full circle from the passage quoted in the preface to this book: 'When a country looks at its fighting forces, it is looking in a mirror; the mirror is a true one and the face that it sees will be its own.' With a coup d'état the reflection comes to life, leaps at the throat of the person facing it; suddenly the mirror is back to front, distorted. The reflection is recreating reality in its own image. The result may not be pretty.

APPENDIX
Coups d'Etat since 1945

1945
Brazil

1947
Ecuador (failed)
Nicaragua
Paraguay (failed)
Thailand

1948
Czechoslovakia
El Salvador
Paraguay
Paraguay
Peru (failed)
Peru
South Korea (failed)
Venezuela

1949
Guatamala (failed)
Panama
Paraguay
Syria
Syria
Syria

1950
Haiti
Indonesia (failed)
Indonesia (failed)
Venezuela (failed)

1951
Argentina (failed)
Panama
Syria
Thailand (failed)
Thailand

1952
Bolivia
Cuba
Egypt

1954
Paraguay
Syria

1955
Argentina (failed)
Argentina
Argentina

Brazil
Guatemala (failed)
Sudan (failed)

1956
Peru (failed)

1958
Burma
France
Iraq
Pakistan
Sudan
Thailand
Venezuela

1959
Iraq (failed)
Sudan (failed)

1960
Argentina (failed)
Congo
Guatemala (failed)
Laos
Nepal
El Salvador
Turkey
Venezuela (failed)

1961
Brazil
Ecuador
Ethiopia (failed)
France (failed)
Lebanon (failed)
El Salvador
South Korea
Syria
Venezuela (failed)

1962
Argentina
Argentina (failed)
Burma
Dominican Republic (failed)
Peru
Sri Lanka (failed)
Syria
Syria (failed)
Turkey (failed)
Venezuela (failed)
Venezuela (failed)
North Yemen

1963
Algeria (failed)
Argentina (failed)
Congo
Dahomey
Dominican Republic
Ecuador
Guatemala
Honduras
Iraq
Iraq (failed)
Iraq
Laos (failed)
Peru
South Vietnam
Syria
Syria (failed)
Togo
Turkey (failed)

1964
Bolivia
Brazil
Gabon (failed)
Laos
Sudan

South Vietnam (failed)

1965
Algeria
Burundi (failed)
Congo
Congo
Dahomey
Dahomey
Indonesia (failed)
Indonesia
Iraq (failed)
South Vietnam (failed)

1966
Argentina
Burundi
Central African Republic
Congo (failed)
Ecuador
Ghana
Indonesia
Iraq (failed)
Nigeria
Nigeria
Rwanda
Syria
Syria (failed)
Upper Volta

1967
Algeria (failed)
Congo (failed)
Dahomey
Ghana (failed)
Greece
Greece (failed)
Nicaragua (failed)
Sierra Leone
Togo
North Yemen

1968
Iraq
Mali
Panama
Peru
Sierra Leone
South Yemen

1969
Bolivia
Congo (failed)
Dahomey
Libya
Panama (failed)
Somalia
South Yemen
Sudan

1970
Bolivia
Cambodia
Syria
Togo (failed)

1971
Argentina
Argentina (failed)
Argentina (failed)
Bolivia (failed)
Morocco (failed)
Sierra Leone (failed)
Sudan
Sudan
Thailand
Turkey
Uganda

1972
Burundi (failed)
Congo (failed)
Dahomey
Ecuador
El Salvador (failed)
Ghana
Morocco (failed)

1973
Afghanistan
Chile (failed)
Chile
Greece
Rwanda
Uruguay

1974
Bolivia (failed)
Bolivia (failed)
Central African Republic (failed)
Cyprus (failed)
Ethiopia
Niger
Portugal (failed)
Portugal
Uganda (failed)
Upper Volta
North Yemen

1975
Bangladesh
Bangladesh
Chad
The Comoros
Dahomey (failed)
Ecuador (failed)
Honduras
Mozambique (failed)
Nigeria
Peru
Sudan (failed)
Turkey (failed)

1976
Afghanistan (failed)
Argentina
Burundi
Chad (failed)
Libya (failed)
Mali (failed)
Niger (failed)
Nigeria (failed)
Thailand
Uruguay

1977
Angola (failed)
Bangladesh (failed)
Benin (failed)
Chad (failed)
Congo (failed)
Ethiopia (failed)
Honduras (failed)
Seychelles
Sudan (failed)
Thailand (failed)
Thailand
Togo

1978
Afghanistan
Bolivia
Bolivia
Cambodia
The Comoros (failed)
The Comoros
Ghana

Honduras
Nicaragua
Pakistan
Seychelles (failed)
North Yemen (failed)
South Yemen (failed)

1979
Afghanistan
Bolivia
Central African Republic
El Salvador
Equatorial Guinea
Ghana
Grenada
Iran
Nicaragua

1980
Bolivia
Guinea-Bissau
Liberia
Mauritania
Rwanda (failed)
Surinam
Turkey
Upper Volta

1981
Bangladesh (failed)
Bolivia
Dominica (failed)
Equatorial Guinea (failed)
Gambia (failed)
Mauritania (failed)
Seychelles (failed)
Sudan (failed)
Surinam (failed)
Thailand (failed)
Upper Volta
Zambia (failed)

1982
Bangladesh
Central African Republic
Ghana
Ghana (failed)
Guatemala
Kenya (failed)
Surinam
Upper Volta

1983
Equatorial Guinea (failed)
Ghana (failed)
Grenada
Guatemala (failed)
Guatemala
Liberia (failed)
Niger (failed)
Nigeria
South Yemen (failed)
Upper Volta
Zaïre (failed)

1984
Bolivia (failed)
Cameroon (failed)
The Comoros (failed)
Ghana (failed)
Guatemala (failed)
Guinea Republic (failed)
Guinea Republic
Iraq (failed)
Upper Volta (failed)

1985
Bahrain (failed)

Bolivia (failed)
Ghana (failed)
Guinea-Bissau (failed)
Guinea Republic (failed)
Guinea Republic (failed)
Liberia (failed)
Nigeria
Nigeria (failed)
Sudan
Sudan (failed)
Thailand (failed)
Uganda
North Yemen (failed)

1986
Haiti
Lesotho
Philippines
Philippines (failed)
Togo (failed)
Uganda
South Yemen

BIBLIOGRAPHY

The list of books and periodicals below represents my 'core' bibliography, that is, the reading material that I found most helpful and to which I referred most often. The number of publications dealing solely (or even in part) with the operational aspects of a given coup d'état is very small, accounting for only a proportion of those listed below. Readers looking for further information on the wider socio-political issues surrounding coups d'état should look closely at the bibliographies in the works I have listed, especially Finer, Luttwak, Decalo and Simon.

Cartwright, J. *Political Leadership in Africa.* Croom Helm, 1983

Davis, N. *The Last Two Years of Salvador Allende.* IB Tauris, 1985

Decalo, S. *Coups and Army Rule In Africa.* Yale University Press, 1980

Dunkerley, J. *Bolivia – Coup d'Etat.* Latin-American Bureau, 1980

Farer, T. J. *War Clouds on the Horn of Africa.* Carnegie Endowment for International Peace, revised edn, 1979

Finer, Professor S. E. *The Man on Horseback.* Peregrine, revised edn, 1976

Forsyth, F. *The Biafra Story.* Severn, revised edn, 1980

— *The Dogs of War.* Corgi, 1975

Geraghty, A. *Who Dares Wins.* Arms & Armour Press, 1980

Girling, J. L. S. *Thailand – Society and Culture.* Cornell University Press, 1981

Hackett, General Sir John. *The Profession of Arms.* Sidgwick & Jackson, 1983

Henissart, P. *Wolves in the City: The Death of French Algeria.* Hart-Davis, 1971

Horne, A. *A Savage War of Peace: Algeria 1954–1962.* Macmillan, 1977

Labin, S. *Chile: The Crime of Resistance.* Foreign Affairs Publishing, 1982

Luttwak, Dr E. *Coup d'Etat; A Practical Manual.* Penguin, 1968

Mancham, J. *Paradise Raped.* Methuen, 1982

Martin, D. *General Amin.* Faber & Faber, 1974

Mockler, A. *The New Mercenaries.* Sidgwick & Jackson, 1985

Pedler, Sir Frederick. *Main Currents of West African History.* Macmillan, 1979

Porch, D. *The Portuguese Armed Forces and the Revolution.* Croom Helm, 1977

Roosevelt, K. *Countercoup – The Struggle for Control of Iran.* McGraw Hill, 1979

Sandford, G., and Vigilante, R. *Grenada: The Untold Story.* Madison, 1984

Simon, S. W. (ed.). *The Military and Security in the Third World.* Westview Press, 1978

Newspapers, journals and periodicals

The Times, Daily Telegraph, The Guardian, The Financial Times, International Herald-Tribune, Newsweek, Time, Africa Now, Africa

Economic Digest, Middle East Economic Digest, Journal of the Royal United Services Institute, Defence Africa and the Middle East, Defensa Latino Americana, International Broadcast Engineer, Defence, Miltronics, International Defence Review, Jane's Defence Weekly, Afrique Défense, Summary of World Broadcasts (BBC, Caversham)

INDEX